The Falmer Press Teachers' Library: 6

Beginning Qualitative Research
A Philosophic and Practical Guide

Pamela Maykut

and

Richard Morehouse

The Falmer Press

(A member of the Taylor & Francis Group)
London • Washington, D.C.

UK   The Falmer Press, 1 Gunpowder Square, London EC4A 3DE
USA   The Falmer Press, Taylor & Francis Inc., 1900 Frost Road, Suite 101, Bristol, PA 19007

First published in 1994
Reprinted 1995, 1996 and 1997

A catalogue record for this book is available from the British Library

Library of Congress Cataloging-in-Publication Data are available on request

ISBN 0 7507 0272 9 cased
ISBN 0 7507 0273 7 paper

Jacket design by Caroline Archer

Typeset in 11/13 pt Garamond by
Graphicraft Typesetters Ltd., Hong Kong

Printed in Great Britain by Biddles Ltd, Guildford and King's Lynn on paper which has a specified pH value on final paper manufacture of not less than 7.5 and is therefore 'acid free'.

Contents

List of Figures, Tables and Research Exercises   vi
Introduction   viii

Part I Building a Philosophic Foundation for Qualitative Research   xiii

1   Philosophic Underpinnings: An Overview   1
2   Before Beginning Research: A Philosophic Perspective   7
3   The Qualitative Posture: Indwelling   25

Part II From Ideas to Outcomes: Conducting Qualitative Research   41

4   Designing Qualitative Research: An Overview   43
5   Generating Ideas   50
6   Building a Sample   56
7   Data Collection In The Natural Setting: Studying
    People, Studying Settings   68

Part III Data Analysis   119

8   Qualitative Data Analysis: An Overview   121
9   Qualitative Data Analysis: Using The Constant
    Comparative Method   126
10 Communicating The Outcomes Of Qualitative Research   150

Appendix   165
Research Proposals   167
Interview Schedule Television and Society   178
Interview Schedule Exploring People's Experience of
    Cross-sex Friendships   184
Index   190

Figures and Tables

Figure 4.1   Characteristics of qualitative research   48

Figure 5.1   Concept maps created by student researchers   51

Figure 6.1   A possible profile for the study example: Understanding more about students' experience of learning from lectures   61

Figure 7.1   Excerpt from the field notes of a student researcher who was able to take notes during the observation   74

Figure 7.2   Map from a middle school cafeteria   76

Figure 7.3   Excerpt from the field notes of a student researcher who recorded her notes after an observation   77

Figure 7.4   General procedure for developing an interview guide or an interview schedule   84

Figure 7.5   An excerpt from the transcript of an in-depth interview conducted by a student researcher   102

Figure 7.6   Group interview guide developed by a student researcher for a qualitative study of prejudice among college students   108

Figure 9.1   Unitizing the data   130

Figure 9.2   Unitizing a long unit of meaning   130

Figure 9.3   Illustration of data analysis process   133

Figure 9.4   Constant comparative method of data analysis   135

Figure 9.5   First provisional coding category   136

Figure 9.6   Continuing provisional coding categories   136

Figure 9.7   Expanding provisional categories   137

Figure 9.8   Adding new categories   138

Table 1.1   Framing research within philosophy   4

Table 2.1   Postulates of the research paradigms   12

Table 2.2   Research characteristics and trends in historic context   14

Research exercise #1: Understanding the role of people's words and actions   19

Research exercise #2: Using your own experience to understand the paradigm shift   20

Research exercise #3: Understanding tacit and explicit knowledge   34

Research exercise #4: Working with ambiguity   36

Research exercise #5: Developing a focus of inquiry   50

Research exercise #6: Exploring the concept of maximum variation   58

Research exercise #7: Developing a beginning guide for sample selection   60

Research exercise #8: Observing without interpreting   77

Research exercise #9: Reconstructing observations from the field   78

Research exercise #10: Beginning the development of an interview   87

Research exercise #11: Developing interview questions   92

Research exercise #12: Drafting an interview guide or an interview schedule   97

Research exercise #13: Planning and conducting a group interview   109

Research exercise #14: Practicing unitizing, categorizing and writing rules for inclusion   142

Acknowledgments

Our path to writing this book has been filled with many teachers. You will meet many of them as you read these pages and see their ideas presented and their names referenced. What you will not see are the names of the many students (graduate and undergraduate) who have delighted us with their interest and enthusiasm for qualitative research and encouraged us by their commitment to exemplary work. We gratefully acknowledge their contribution to our learning.

P.M. and R.M.

Introduction

Qualitative research is a growing enterprise worldwide. It is perhaps most widely accepted in England, Australia, and the Scandinavian countries. It is growing but less well accepted in the United States and Canada. Qualitative research methods are particularly well developed in the sociology and anthropology of education. In the United States, and to some degree Canada, educational research is dominated by a psychological agenda and by experimental methods. Psychologists in North America are beginning to use qualitative methods in their research as it relates to educational issues and the understanding of learning and cognition. However, the psychology of learning, with its roots in behaviorism and the experimental method, has resisted or perhaps more accurately ignored, any examination of qualitative research methods. Teacher preparation in the United States continues to have a psychological approach and to value quantitative research studies and to undervalue qualitative research methods. While it is true that the American Educational Research Association (AERA) has made a place for qualitative research, an unsystematic look at AERA journals and convention programs over the last ten years continues to demonstrate the dominance of quantitative studies. An interesting observation is that AERA conventions and journals appear to have more papers, panels and articles *about* qualitative methods than they do papers, panels and articles that report research *using* qualitative methods. This may be an indication that qualitative research methods, at least in the United States, are still fighting for an equal footing with quantitative research methods. On the other hand, articles on quantitative methods tend to be about new statistical methods and meta-analysis, not articles that defend or examine basic points regarding quantitative methods.

It is within this context that *Beginning Qualitative Research: A Philosophic and Practical Guide* is written. We found that our students in psychology and education understood the orientation, the approach, the *modus operandi* of quantitative methods but not those used by qualitative researchers. Typical students in psychology or education or working teachers at an inservice meeting have a comfort level with quantitative research findings even if they might not know much about how to conduct a quantitative study or even feel confident about their understanding or interpretation of the statistical nature of the findings. These students and teachers express the opinion that experimental studies are truly scientific and that non-experimental studies are the same as anecdotal incidents and cannot be taken seriously by psychologists, by teachers, or by educational administrators. As teachers of both quantitative and qualitative research methods, we have observed an interesting paradox in many of the students in our classes and teachers with whom we work: they state, sometimes explicitly, that because they can understand qualitative studies better than they can understand quantitative/experimental studies, they are uncertain of the rigor of qualitative studies. Since these studies are understandable, these beginning researchers fear that their senior colleagues or school administrators might not take these studies seriously. They further fear that their findings may not be considered important. These teachers and students express the view that they are unsure about the scientific value of qualitative studies they have read because they can understand them. They see serious research as something which is beyond their understanding, at least without extensive study. These teachers and students equate their lack of knowledge about experimental statistical studies as being synonymous with rigor and acceptance by a distant and unapproachable scientific other. This connection between understanding and rigor is compounded by the lack of extended methods sections in popular works in psychology and education such as Carol Gilligan's *In a Different Voice* (1982) and Mary Belenky and her colleagues' *Women's Ways of Knowing* (1986). These two works, while contributing much to the interest in women's perspectives on knowledge and morality and to a general interest in what can be understood via qualitative methods, have done little to add to the general public understanding of qualitative research as a rigorous and acceptable way of doing serious research.

Classroom teachers, in particular, state that they cannot defend qualitative research to their administrators because these administrators do not see the research as rigorous or 'scientific'. Psychology students, especially undergraduate psychology students, see little qualitative research cited in their text books. General psychology books and research methods books directed at undergraduate students in the United States are cursory, if not downright dismissive, in their discussion of qualitative methods, often lumping all qualitative research under the heading of case studies.

In addition to understanding that qualitative research can be both understandable and rigorous, beginning qualitative researchers also need hands-on experience with data analysis. Data analysis may well be the heart of qualitative research. It is one of the places that qualitative research is most different from quantitative research methods. As data analysis is so central to doing qualitative research, we choose to spend little time on the computer programs that may be used effectively by experienced researchers. It is our thinking that to understand qualitative data analysis methods as unique and as rigorous, it is important for beginning qualitative researchers to 'eyeball' the data. Our experience indicates that this may even be true of students in beginning quantitative research methods courses. If students, as they begin exploring quantitative research, only see the statistical results as they come to them from the computer screen, they do not have a clear understanding of these results even though they have spent a semester studying statistics. Therefore, our focus in this book is on a hands-on and transparent method of doing qualitative research analysis. In the data analysis sections of the book, we attempt to make the process of data analysis and its philosophic underpinnings visible to the beginning researchers. The idea about making process visible in the data analysis sections, and throughout the entire book, is one of the hallmarks of our efforts. It is the way we attempt to connect the philosophic underpinnings with the practical guide. If we succeed in that effort, it is to the extent that the philosophic underpinnings are clearly stated and the connections with the philosophy are visible. We think that computer-assisted data analysis may make the connections to the philosophic underpinning less clear and, therefore, the understanding of the beginning researcher of the nature of the process less solid. What we call transparency is a technique for teaching and learning that aids learning by connecting teaching with learning via visible markers so that teacher and student can move back and forth across the material being learned; observing appropriate moves and correcting inappropriate ones (Morehouse, 1985; 1987; 1988).

Who should read this book? Who will gain most by reading it? Those readers who are steeped in the quantitative or experimental tradition within psychology and education but who are looking for answers to questions they are not getting from these methods. Also, teachers and students of psychology or cognitive studies who are trying to understand a phenomena rather than looking to find cause and effect may gain new insights from this work.

Other readers who are already schooled in the ways of qualitative research or who have read widely in the sociology and anthropology of education may not find this book as helpful, though some may find the examination of the philosophic differences between the quantitative and qualitative approach somewhat instructive. Our concern, however, is with readers who have grown up in a culture dominated by one scientific method, the method of experimental and quantitative research and who are looking to find their way as beginning researchers.

These readers, we believe, will benefit not only from the philosophic perspective at the beginning of the book but also by the practical suggestions in the second half of the book, as these strategies and methods are built on the philosophic underpinnings and further provide the perspective qualitative researcher with an orientation for doing research. Further, these readers will be able to explain their research initiatives to school administrators and colleagues who are steeped in the experimental perspective. Further, and perhaps most importantly, they can feel confident in themselves as researchers.

The audience for the book, therefore, is likely to be an undergraduate or graduate student in psychology, a student in teacher preparation or a classroom teacher in North America. Serious researchers will, after a while, move beyond this beginning work. If students and classroom teachers find that their understanding of qualitative methods and its place within psychological and educational research has been sufficient to get them started in several research projects and hungering for more knowledge about methods and their philosophic underpinning then, we will have succeeded.

We have attempted to make the philosophic as well as the practical elements of the book assessable to a wide audience. Our hope is that *Beginning Qualitative Research: A Philosophic and Practical Guide* will be available to a diverse audience including teachers, teacher educators, school administrators, and students in psychology and education, thus making the tools of qualitative research available to a large group of diverse people and contributing to informed discussions between administrators and teachers, college students and research faculty members and qualitative and quantitative researchers.

References

BELENKY, M., CLINCHY, B., GOLDBERGER, N. and TARULE, J. (1986) Women's Ways of Knowing, New York: Basic.

GILLIGAN, C. (1982) In a Different Voice: Psychological Theory and Women's Development, Cambridge, MA: Harvard University Press.

MOREHOUSE, R. (1985) 'Transcript analysis and teacher training', *Analytic Teaching*, **5**, 2, pp. 18–22.

Morehouse, R. (1987) 'Curiosity and Transparency: Uncovering Process', The Second Decade: Conference on Philosophy for Children at Texas Wesleyan College, Fort Worth, TX (Unpublished).

Morehouse, R. (1988) 'Tools for improving student discussion or helping students and teachers create a community of inquiry', *Analytic Teaching*, **8**, 2, pp. 56–63.

Part I

Building a Philosophic Foundation for Qualitative Research

Chapter 1

Philosophic Underpinnings: An Overview

This book begins with an introduction to the philosophic underpinnings that shape our understanding of the qualitative research enterprise. A philosophic orientation to inquiry will aid you in forming a frame of reference about the nature of qualitative inquiry and help you form a platform upon which to build a hands-on practical guide for conducting a qualitative research project from beginning to end. Our goal in the philosophic section is to *get you to think differently about doing research before you begin doing research*. This goes against the trend of most books on qualitative research which begin with a presentation of methods for conducting research (Berg, 1989; Bogdan and Taylor, 1975; Burgess, 1985; Patton, 1990), or at most a brief history of qualitative inquiry (Bogdan and Biklen, 1982). On the other hand, Kincheloe (1991) presents a philosophic perspective on qualitative research but frames it more or less exclusively within the context of teacher empowerment and provides little practical help for the beginning researcher. It is our firm belief that a frame of reference built on an understanding of the philosophic underpinning of quantitative and qualitative research is essential for the beginning qualitative researcher.

An understanding of the philosphic assumptions is important as one begins a research project because questions will come up that were not, perhaps could not be, anticipated. These unanticipated questions demand answers, often immediate answers. If a problem occurs while one is gathering data, there is no time to go back and check notes or to review a research article. Our first inclination when facing a new problem is to fall back on what we know best, and what we know best about research are the models presented by traditional science.

While the learning-by-doing approach appears to have the advantage of getting the beginning researcher into a research project quickly and therefore providing a practical way to develop an understanding of research, it also has some serious disadvantages. A philosophic framework is particularly important for the beginning qualitative researcher as differences in the way qualitative and quantitative researchers approach research appear not only on the surface where they can be easily detected, but also on very basic levels that cannot be easily noticed if one does not understand the assumptions that underscore the research practices. Without an understanding of these underpinnings, many of us see any research problems as variations of quantitative inquiry, that is, we think in terms of the null hypothesis, objective data collection, reliability and validity. Metaphorically, we tend to see new things with the older, more established blueprints in our minds. Another potential problem of not having a sense of the philosophic underpinnings of qualitative and quantitative research is the inability to make a strong case for conducting a qualitative research project in that particular situation and/or setting. If the researcher cannot articulate, at least to herself, the reasons for using qualitative methods in a research project, it is likely that she will be unable to defend the project as a rigorous and valued piece of scholarship. The better one understands the larger picture that qualitative research methods fit into, the better one can conduct research within the research tradition that one is working within. As qualitative research is still a minority voice, it needs strong defenders.

Our experience as researchers and teachers of research has taught us that a philosophic perspective is helpful to the beginning researcher even though they may initially fight the idea of examining philosophical underpinnings of the major research traditions. Beginning qualitative researchers need all the help they can get as they swim against the tide of cultural heritage of how science is done. While the current is less strong than it was a few years ago, it is still powerful. By presenting a philosophic perspective in these first chapters, we hope to reshape your basic frame of reference. We plan to steep you in an alternate point of view, so as to counter-balance the traditional way of answering research questions. Without the philosophic background beginning qualitative researchers are left without the conceptual tools to think through problems and issues as they arise.

Quantitative research is based on observations that are converted into discrete units that can be compared to other units by using statistical analysis. While there may be modifications and variations on this general picture of quantitative research, statistical analysis is an essential part of quantitative research. Qualitative research, on the other hand, generally examines people's words and actions in narrative or descriptive ways more closely representing the situation as experienced by the participants. These surface differences between quantitative and qualitative research are further distinguished by their philosophic underpinnings.

Qualitative research is based on a phenomenological position, while quantitative research is based on a positivist position. To explore the differences between qualitative and quantitative inquiry from a philosophic perspective a common philosophic vocabulary is helpful.

Building a Philosophic Vocabulary for Understanding Qualitative and Quantitative Inquiry

A common vocabulary is necessary to explore the philosophic assumptions of the two research positions. Positivism and phenomenology are the two overarching perspectives that shape our understanding of research. The word *positivism* was first coined by Auguste Comte as early as the 1830s and for Comte positivism was synonymous with science or with positive or observable facts (Stromberg, 1986). Within the larger discussion of the history of science, positivism has come to mean objective inquiry based on measurable variables and provable propositions. The positivist research orientation holds that science is or should be primarily concerned with the explanation and the prediction of observable events (Kincheloe, 1991). It is the insistence on explanation, prediction, and proof that are the hallmarks of positivism.

Phenomenological approach is a focus on understanding the meaning events have for persons being studied (Patton, 1991). The phenomenological approach to inquiry includes qualitative research but also has under its umbrella such areas in inquiry as ethnomethodology, symbolic interactionism, hermeneutic inquiry, grounded theory, naturalist inquiry, and ethnography (Patton, 1991). Phenomenology, like positivism, should be seen in historic context. Two important authors who have articulated the phenomenological position are Maurice Merleau-Ponty (1962) and Michael Polanyi (1962; 1967; Polanyi and Prosch, 1975). The phenomenological position see the individual and his or her world as co-constituted. 'In the truest sense, the person is viewed as having no existence apart from the world, and the world as having no existence apart from the person' (Valle and King, 1978).

To sort out and gain a more detailed picture of the differences, a series of questions is proposed. These questions can be placed into four philosophical categories. The areas of questions concern ontology, epistemology, logic, and teleology. Ontological assumptions concern questions about the nature of reality. One key ontological question is: What is the nature of reality? Epistemological assumptions concern the origins of knowledge. What is the relationship between the knower and the known? What role do values play in understanding? are important epistemological questions. Logic deals with principles of demonstration

Table 1.1: Framing research within philosophy

Areas of Philosophy as They Relate to Research	Questions
1 Ontology raises questions about the nature of reality.	What is the nature of the world? What is real? What counts as evidence?
2 Epistemology is interested in the origins and nature of knowing and the construction of knowledge.	What is the relationship between the knower and the known? What role do values play in understanding?
3 Logic, as it relates to research, deals with principles of demonstration and verification.	Are causal links between bits of information possible?
4 Teleology is generally concerned with questions of purpose.	What is research for?

or verification. Important questions about the logic of inquiry are: Are causal linkages between bits of information possible? What is the possibility of generalization? Teleological questions include: What does research contribute to knowledge? What is the purpose of research?

The answers to these questions make up what we call the postulates of the research paradigms. Before examining these postulates two other words need clarification: *paradigm* and *postulates*. A paradigm has come to mean a set of overarching and interconnected assumptions about the nature of reality. The word *assumptions* is key. One must make assumptions, for example, about the nature of reality, because anything that a researcher might do to test what reality is must be based on some understanding of that reality. A philosophic assumption cannot be proved but may be stipulated; these stipulations we call postulates. Our definition of a postulate is an assumption stated positively. A set of postulates make up a paradigm. The paradigm, like the postulates on which it is based, cannot itself be tested; the paradigm provides the basis on which we build our verifiable knowledge.

The relationship between methods, traditions, postulates, and paradigms is a complex one. A paradigm provides the largest framework within which research takes place. It is the world view within which researchers work. Postulates are the individual assumptions that are stipulated to be true. A tradition, as we use the term, consists of more or less like-minded researchers who accept the postulates within the paradigm as working assumptions. Research methods, on the other hand, are many and varied within that tradition. While the research methods are distinctive, the methods share some specific points and more importantly a general orientation within the tradition. In this case, the two competing traditions are the positivist and the phenomenological traditions.

We take a radical position on the nature of qualitative research and its relationship to traditional research arguing that qualitative research is based on a fundamentally different set of postulates than is the dominant or positivist tradition on research. Our position has important implications for research. It means, among other things, that one must carefully match research questions with methods of collecting and analyzing data. One set of postulates constitutes what we call an alternate paradigm and the phenomenological approach to inquiry, while another set of postulates frames the dominant paradigm and positivist approach. In the next chapter, a side-by-side comparison of the positivist and phenomenological approaches to research will be presented along with an overview of the history of the research traditions.

Overview of Philosophical Chapters within the Context of the Rest of the Book

The next chapter provides a comparison of the positivist and the phenomenological positions of inquiry. These positions are placed within historic context to further aid the prospective researcher in understanding the perspective within which they will be working. The detailed comparison for the phenomenological and the positivist approach to inquiry will not only help to distinguish the two traditions from each other but will also highlight the common ground shared by the various methods within the phenomenological tradition. Further, this comparison will lay the ground work for the specific approach to phenomenological inquiry developed here — a qualitative research method.

Chapter 3 explicates an important philosophic orientation within qualitative research, that is, indwelling. Indwelling is neither philosophy nor method. It is rather what we call a posture. A posture is state or condition in relationship to other persons or situations. A posture in this sense is a way of being. We see the posture of indwelling as central to our understanding of qualitative research.

These two chapters set up a background, develop a common vocabulary, and establish a philosophic basis upon which the methods of doing qualitative research are built. The research methods chapters are practical and straightforward but built on the philosophic basis of the first two chapters.

References

BERG, B. (1989) *Qualitative Research Methods for the Social Sciences*, Boston, MA: Allyn and Bacon.

BOGDAN, R. and TAYLOR, S. (1975) *Introduction to Qualitative Research Methods: A Phenomenological Approach to the Social Sciences*, New York: Wiley.

BOGDAN, R. and BIKLEN, S. (1982) *Qualitative Research for Education: An Introduction to Theory and Methods*, Boston, MA: Allyn and Bacon.

BURGESS, R. (Ed) (1985) *Strategies of Educational Research: Qualitative Methods*, London: Falmer.

KINCHELOE, J. (1991) *Teachers as Researchers: Qualitative Inquiry as a Path to Empowerment*, London: Falmer.

MERLEAU-PONTY, M. (1962) *Phenomenology of Perception* (SMITH, C. Trans.), London: Routledge and Kegan Paul. (Originally published 1962).

PATTON, M.J. (1991) 'Qualitative research on college students: Philosophical and methodological comparisons with the quantitative approach', *Journal of College Student Development* **32**, pp. 389–96.

POLANYI, M. (1962) *Personal knowledge: Toward a Post-critical Philosophy*, Chicago, IL: The University of Chicago.

POLANYI, M. (1967) *The Tacit Dimension*, New York: Anchor Books.

POLANYI, M. and PROSCH, H. (1975) *Meaning*, Chicago, IL: University of Chicago.

STROMBERG, R. (1986) *European Intellectual History since 1789* (4th ed.), Englewood Cliffs, NJ: Prentice-Hall.

VALLE, R. and KING, M. (Eds) (1978) *Existential Phenomenological Alternatives for Psychology*, New York: Oxford University.

Chapter 2

Before Beginning Research: A Philosophic Perspective

Why is qualitative research and not quantitative research in the minority status? Why is it necessary to present a philosophic perspective on qualitative research and not on quantitative research? While this is not the place to present an extended history of research, let us just say that when experimental methods were first introduced as a challenge to the scholastic methods, a rigorous and philosophic defense of the experimental methods were required. Qualitative methods still face that challenge, because the philosophic underpinnings are not widely understood. If the underlying philosophy is not understood, the new orientation, in this case qualitative research, is seen as a less rigorous and less valued way of doing inquiry.

For good or ill, the human sciences, as seen by the positivists, have often taken their lead from physics and chemistry. This connection to the natural sciences, from at least the time of Newton, has been dominated by a belief in objective observation, quantifiable data and verifiable truths. Evelyn Fox Keller in *Reflections on Gender and Science* (1985) argues that this way of doing science is related to a patriarchal view of the world. We support Fox's position that the patriarchal view of science has marginalized all ways of doing science which are not like the ways that natural science has been traditionally done, that is, any non-experimental, non-objective ways of doing science. Recently, this newer view of science has been challenged by new ways of doing natural science (especially physics), feminist theory, and post-modern sensibilities (Habermas, 1989; Heisenberg, 1958; Keller, 1985; West, 1989). These alternate voices have contributed to making qualitative research an acceptable way of doing science. At the same time that these perspectives were beginning to be articulated, other challenges were mounted on the traditional methods within educational research (Campbell, 1975; Stake, 1978).

Historically, qualitative research can be seen as marginalized in both its participants (subjects as defined by traditional science) and by its methodology. We will begin by looking at the participants of early qualitative studies. Cultural anthropologists were among the first and best known qualitative researchers. Until recently anthropologists studied 'primitive' peoples almost exclusively. While anthropologists often argued that the participants in their studies should not be considered primitive, they continued their almost exclusive examination of these participants and therefore kept their subjects marginalized. Freud and Piaget, whom we would include under the broad category of qualitative researchers, studied neurotic women and children respectively: Two groups on the margins of the male patriarchal scientific culture. The Chicago School of Sociology studied street gangs and institutionalized persons. More recently, qualitative methods have been used to study the educational process in elementary, secondary and university settings. As a part of the look at education and students, William Perry (1970) examined the intellectual and moral changes in Harvard males and, by studying a group of persons valued by the dominant society, helped to move qualitative research closer to the center of serious research.

Qualitative research methods also began at the margins of acceptable science. From Freud on, qualitative researchers have been presenting their findings in language which did not directly challenge the traditional ways of doing science. Anthropologists, for example, did not even suggest that their method might be used by other social science disciplines. Freud, as a medical doctor, wrote case studies and, while using the knowledge gained from his work with patients as a part of his theory building, he placed his theories within a medical or literary context, rather than making his case from a careful examination of his case studies. In fact, it is not until the pioneering work of Carl Rogers that transcripts of therapy were brought out for public inspection (Rogers, 1942; 1951). From a different perspective, Piaget's clinical interview method began to break into mainstream science with the power of his theoretical work, rather than by a solid presentation of his method. Developmental psychologists such as Mary Ainsworth (1979) have examined mother-child relationships using qualitative methods but have not made a strong case for a qualitative approach. It is surprising that methods until very recently have not been presented as a part of the research reports; the reader was left in the dark about how the researcher came to the conclusion that she did.

In fact, it is difficult to re-evaluate older qualitative studies by examining the way the researchers analyzed their data. Even recent qualitative studies such as *Women's Ways of Knowing* (Belenky, Clinchy, Goldberger and Tarule, 1985) and *In a Different Voice* (Gilligan, 1982) provided little methodological information. One is left with the impression that there are no rigorous ways of collecting and analyzing qualitative data—qualitative research, one is led to believe by this lack of information, must be intuitive, and perhaps qualitative methods are not a part of good science.

As we will show shortly, this is not the case. But before making the case for a rigorous qualitative methodology, we will briefly look at Kuhn's view of the sociology of science as it relates to qualitative research.

Paradigms and Research

To further our understanding of the current status of qualitative research, we will briefly examine the implications of Thomas Kuhn's *The Structure of Scientific Revolutions* (1962) and extend Kuhn's argument by placing research methods within this framework. Kuhn (1962) first introduced the concept of paradigm into the history and sociology of science. Kuhn discusses two phases or periods of research in science: normal and revolutionary. Research during periods of normal science can be thought of as solving a puzzle within a general pattern already outlined by the major theories of that science. As more and more of the pieces of the puzzle are put together, Kuhn argues, some of them do not fit. In other words, a researcher might find out some new bits of information which have been verified by the methods of the science but which do not fit into the prevailing paradigms. Kuhn calls these misfit bits of information and research findings anomalies. As a researcher finds data which are verified using acceptable methods but that do not support existing theories, it becomes more and more difficult to support those theories. The reason for this is that a theory is held together by the way in which all or most of the the data about that question supports the larger picture.

The relationship between theory, postulates, and paradigms is a complex one. While Kuhn's work on the history of science is widely known, what is less widely known is that a major shift has to also occur in the methodology of science, in the way science is researched. Kuhn's ideas regarding normal and revolutionary science should also be applied to the research methods of a discipline. The dominant method of science today we will refer to as the traditional method.

Yvonna Lincoln and Egon Guba's *Naturalistic Inquiry* (1985), which is elaborate in detail and comprehensive in its scope, plays an important role in the recognition of qualitative research as a legitimate way of doing research. They articulate the points raised by Kuhn regarding the shift in research methods within the history of science. Lincoln and

Guba's contribution to the acceptance of qualitative methods within the research community is extended by their articulation of the methodology of qualitative research in a rigorous way, taking their lead from an understanding of changes within the 'hard' sciences. They present qualitative research as a part of an emerging research paradigm which includes lessons taken from theoretical physics and mathematics. Lincoln and Guba work toward placing qualitative research on an equal footing with traditional scientific approaches (cf. Maxwell, 1990a; 1990b; Lincoln, 1990).

Lincoln and Guba (1985) present the philosophical basis for qualitative research as well as a set of techniques and methods for conducting research based on the implications of the new paradigm. Lincoln and Guba take a radical position on the nature of qualitative research and its relationship to traditional research arguing effectively that qualitative research is based on a fundamentally different set of axioms or postulates than is the dominant approach to research, that is, the positivists' position on research. This new set of assumptions or postulates constitutes what we call the alternate paradigm, that is, a paradigm for conducting research which is not yet fully developed.

Lincoln and Guba (1985) and others (Hesse, 1980; Schwartz & Ogilvy, 1979) call this traditional method the positivist paradigm. However, there is also an emerging approach to understanding the world which we call the qualitative approach and which Lincoln and Guba call the emerging paradigm (1985). Each of these approaches or paradigms to research is built on a very different set of underlying assumptions which are outlined below.

Postulates and Paradigms

The postulates of a research paradigm are regarded as self-evident truths in times of normal science (Kuhn, 1962). However, they are not self-evident during periods of rapid change or when there is a shift from one paradigm toward another. Postulates are only self-evident if there is not a competing frame of reference. A postulate, specifically, is something that is stipulated, that is, something given the status of acceptance in order to get on with the task at hand. The value of a postulate to restate is that it provides the bedrock on which to conduct research. O'Donohue (1989), in an article exploring new ways for training clinical psychologists, discusses the role of metaphysics in a similar way as Lincoln and Guba discuss the role of postulates under the name axioms.[1] O'Donohue states that a few metaphysical assumptions (read postulates), though untestable themselves, provide a plausible foundation for doing research. These research methods are directly dependent on the untestable postulate for their legitimacy (O'Donohue, 1989: 1461).

The table below presents six questions about the nature of reality and ways of conducting research. These questions are answered by a set of postulates that make a claim for a way of conducting research. These postulates shape the way researchers approach problems, the methods they use to collect and analyze data, as well as the type of problems they choose to investigate. Table 2.1 lists the most salient differences between the two competing paradigms. The questions in the left column are central to solving problems which present themselves in planning a research project, analyzing the data, and in writing up the results of any study. The six philosophic questions in column one provide the basis for Table 2.1 which provides a capsule view of the different approaches to inquiry.

In discussing dominant paradigm and positivist position, we will use dominant paradigm and positivist position interchangeably and quantitative research resulting from the postulates of that paradigm. The alternate paradigm and the phenomenological position will also be used more or less interchangeably with qualitative research which follows from the postulates within that paradigm. A brief discussion of the postulates as they apply to qualitative research will extend our understanding of how the assumptions of the paradigm affect the outlook and behavior of the researcher. One rarely thinks about the nature of reality because in our day-to-day activities reality is a given. However, as Table 2.1 shows, to ask 'How does the world work?' as a philosophic question about reality affects the way we do research as well as other less rigorous forms of inquiry.

The way we understand the nature of reality directly affects the way we see ourselves in relation to knowledge. If knowledge can be separated into parts and examined individually, it follows that the knower or the researcher can stand apart from who or what he is examining. On the other hand, if knowledge is constructed, then the knower cannot be totally separated from what is known: The world is co-constituted. It follows from Postulate II that researchers within the two paradigms ask different questions and approach research in different ways.

In like manner, the researcher's understanding of causal links stems from the three postulates which come before it (Alternate paradigm I). If reality is multiple and constructed, it follows that the causal links will be mutual (that is, constructed) and that in terms of what an event of action means, the event is not unidirectional but multidirectional. This

Table 2.1: Postulates of the research paradigms

Questions	Postulates of the positivist approach (The dominant paradigm)	Postulates of the phenomenological approach (An alternate paradigm)
I. How does the world work?	Reality is one. By carefully dividing and studying its parts, the whole can be understood.	There are multiple realities. These realities are socio-psychological constructions forming an interconnected whole. These realities can only be understood as such.
II. What is the relationship between the knower and the known?	The knower can stand outside of what is to be known. True objectivity is possible.	The knower and the known are interdependent.
III. What role do values play in understanding the world?	Values can be suspended in order to understand.	Values mediate and shape what is understood.
IV. Are causal linkages possible?	One event comes before another event and can be said to cause that event.	Events shape each other. Multidirectional relationships can be discovered.
V. What is the possibility of generalization?	Explanations from one time and place can be generalized to other times and places.	Only tentative explanations for one time and place are possible.
VI. What does research contribute to knowledge?	Generally, the positivist seeks verification or proof of propositions	Generally, the phenomenologist seeks to discover or uncover propositions.

These postulates undergird different approaches to inquiry.

| Quantitative research approach | Qualitative research approach |

Liberally adapted from Lincoln and Guba, 1985

perspective also has implications for how one looks at data or information which is gathered in the process of research. The qualitative researcher seeks patterns which come out of or emerge from the data. The quantitative researcher makes a guess or forms a hypothesis which is then used to test the data.

Values, the topic discussed in Postulate III, once again can be understood from the postulates which come before it. Values are embedded in the research, embedded in the topic chosen for examination, in the way the researcher examines the topic and in the researcher him or herself. If reality is constructed and the knower and the known are inseparable, then values come with the turf. On the other hand, if the world can be divided into parts and if the knower can stand outside of what is to be known than research can be value free.

Postulate IV asks about cause. The phenomenological approach views events as mutually shaped. Multidirectional relationships can be discovered within situations. Causes are not a prime focus as they are for positivist approach research. Causality is central to the dominant paradigm.

These two hypothetical researchers would, for example, look at the generalizations of their findings (Postulate V) very differently. Qualitative researchers value context sensitivity, that is, understanding a phenomena in all its complexity and within a particular situation and environment. The quantitative researchers works to eliminate all of the unique aspects of the environment in order to apply the results to the largest possible number of subjects and experiments.

Finally, one would expect different contributions to a body of knowledge (Postulate VI) given the intricate connection between and among the postulates. The positivist position on research has never been able to adequately explain how new knowledge is discovered. The positivist approach is oriented toward verifying what has been already discovered by other methods. The alternate paradigm, and the phenomenological position within it, is oriented toward discovery of salient propositions. Discovery of propositions by observation and the careful inspection of the patterns which emerge from the data are the hallmark of the phenomenological approach.

The complexity of things become apparent with attempts at explanation. The above discussion is illustrative: While the alternate paradigm looks to multidirectional, mutually shaped realities in order to explain them and to get individual points to stand out, methods such as tables are effective even though a table is also an organizational model for the traditional paradigm. It is important to realize that while the postulates of the positivist position are seen by their proponents as

Table 2.2: Research characteristics and trends in historic context

Research Characteristic	Dominant Paradigm	Alternate Paradigm
World View	Simple ⟶	Complex
Organization of information	Hierarchic ⟶	Heterarchic
Forms of relationships	Mechanical ⟶	Holographic
Sources of Change	Determined ⟶	Indeterminate
Explanation	Linear causal ⟶	Mutual causal
Nature of change	Assembly ⟶	Morphogenesis
Observer perspective	Objective ⟶	Perspectival

Adapted from Lincoln and Guba, 1985

sequential and divisible into part, the postulates of the phenomenological position should be seen as interconnected and multidirectional.

Placing the research paradigms within a larger picture, Lincoln and Guba (1985) build on the work of Peter Schwartz and James Ogilvy in *The Emergent Paradigm: Changing Patterns of Thought and Belief* (1979). Lincoln and Guba argue that research methods are also subject to paradigm changes. They present an overview of the changing ways the research community views the underlying assumptions upon which research is based. Seven major characteristics are cited by Schwartz and Ogilvy as characteristics of the alternate position that are virtually dia- metrically opposed to those of the traditional position. Table 2.2 above illustrates the major characteristics and the trends which these researchers see. As the table indicates, many researchers see a paradigm shift occur- ring; they see a move from a traditional world-view toward an alternate world-view (Lincoln and Guba, 1985; O'Donohue, 1989; Schwartz and Ogilvy, 1979).

To better understand this paradigm shift let us explore briefly each of the research characteristics and their respective positions. The domi- nate paradigm, or the positivist position, sees the world as simple or at least potentially simple if it can be examined properly and broken apart correctly. In direct contrast, the phenomenological approach sees the world as complex and interconnected, thus research must maintain the complexity if the explanation is to be trustworthy. Next, the dominant paradigm's approach to research sees information organized in hierar- chies, that is, something is always at the bottom (subordinate) and something is always at the top (superordinate). The phenomenological position on research sees information organized in heterarchies. A web of meaning is a good metaphor for a heterarchial organization of infor- mation. Closely related are the forms of relationships. Mechanical forms of relationships characterize the traditional approach. These relationships (metaphorically) can be represented by a one-way flow chart. A holographic image is an appropriate metaphor for understanding the forms of relationships in the alternate position. A holographic reproduction is a three dimensional reproduction. Further, to alter or distort one part of the holographic image is to change the entire image. It is the interconnection of the parts of the relationship which distinguishes a holographic form of a relationship from a mechanical one.

An understanding of the differences between mechanical and holographic relationships is increased by looking at the sources of change and explanation, the next two characteristics to be presented. These two characteristics can only be understood by looking at them together. The traditional approach sees the sources of change as determined and potentially identifiable, while researchers using the alternate approach see the sources of change as indeterminate and therefore not identifiable. In like manner, researchers using the traditional approach explain their findings as linearly causal, that is, *A* causes *B*. The alternate position on causality is that it is mutual, that is, *A* and *B* cause each other. The cause is inseparable from the effect, and further, it is indistinguishable from it.

The difference between the two positions continues regarding the nature of change. The phenomenological position is called morphogenesis while the traditional position is called the mechanical model. Morphogenesis can be understood as the way a living organism develops from a single undifferentiated cell to a complex differentiated multicelled being. Morphogenesis differs from a mechanical model which is assembled one piece at a time. The two positions offer a clear difference regarding the nature of change. To change by morphogenesis is to change organically, with one subtle change affected by the next change in a connected and organic manner. To change mechanically is to change by replacing parts — individual and discrete parts. The observer's perspective is the last distinction between the two orientations. In the positivist approach to research the observer or the observer's instruments are objective or potentially objective. In the phenomenological position the observer is perspectival, that is, has a singular perspective.

The differences between the two paradigms are basic and affect both the general approach to research and particular practices within each research tradition. Michael Polanyi provides a clear statement of the purpose of the positivist position on research when he states: 'The avowed purpose of the positivist sciences is to establish complete intellectual control over experience in terms of precise rules. Further, we should only have to follow the rules faithfully to understand this world'

(Polanyi, 1958). The alternate approach, conversely, can be characterized by a close examination of people's words, actions, and documents in order to discern patterns of meaning which come out of this data.

As the above tables indicate, there is not one scientific method, but at least two scientific methods. However, students and others tend to think of one scientific method that includes such things as experimental and control groups, variables that are quantified, tests for reliability, and large random samples. This method (the traditional approach) is associated with the natural sciences, such as (physics and chemistry, and given high marks because of this association. The traditional scientific method is further equated with generating a hypothesis, testing it, and generalizing the findings to the larger population. In addition to the methodological association, subtler associations are also made with research and the scientific method: the white lab coat — a quintessential scientific badge, the complex and therefore important mathematical formula, and the tests for significance which are confused with indicators of importance. As the working assumptions embedded within the traditional approaches to science affect beginning researchers, it becomes all the more important that they have a solid grounding in the philosophic underpinnings of qualitative research.

These two paradigms are based on two different and competing ways of understanding the world. As we observe and understand, these competing ways of comprehending the world are reflected in the way research data is collected (words versus numbers) and the perspective of the researcher (perspectival versus objective). There are many sources of problems one encounters during the course of a research project. We will focus on three pervasive sources to illustrate the value of understanding the philosophical underpinnings of the research traditions: problems arising from a focus on words rather than numbers, problems relating to perspectival point of view versus objective point of view, and the difference between proof and discovery.

Three Research Issues

These three types of issues will be approached by developing a philosophic perspective, and will provide a preview of the manner in which a philosophic disposition will be integrated throughout the book. The problems to be discussed are specifically: (a) understanding similarities and differences between words and numbers in the two different approaches to research; b) a perspectival observer versus objective observer; and c) discovery versus proof. Each of these areas will be explored in turn and a research exercise will be provided.

Words and numbers

Qualitative research places emphasis on understanding through look-ing closely at people's words, actions and records. The traditional or quantitative approach to research looks past these words, actions and records to their mathematical significance. The traditional approach to research quantifies the results of these observations. Mathematics, or more specifically statistics, plays an important part in the shaping of this view of science. A major difference between the two approaches is not the counting or lack of counting of the occurrences of a particular word or behavior, but rather the meaning given to the words, behaviors or documents as interpreted through quantitative analysis or statistical analysis as apposed to patterns of meaning which emerge from the data and are often presented in the participants' own words.

The statistical view of science came to dominate the way we think about doing science about 75 years ago. The discipline of statistics has articulated these ideas over the course of many years but an under-standing of the underlying philosophy of numbers as they relate to conducting research in both the natural and social sciences has been obscured by the gradual development of the discipline of statistics and, as a result, much of the context and therefore the meaning of statistics is no longer easily visible to researchers as they examine the nature of their paradigm. These methods which were first presented within the philosophy of mathematics have become systematized into a discipline of statistics. Polanyi (1958), while exploring the nature of objectivity in scientific investigation, cites two important works on the use of statis-tics: J.M. Keynes' Treatise on Probability published in 1921 and Sir Ronald Fisher's treatise on the design of experiments written in 1935.

Statistics now appears to be unconnected to its philosophical origins. It is important, however, to recall that there is a long tradition within the history of science concerning the understanding of numbers: what they mean, how to use them, when to use one particular approach and when another.

The philosophic writing in qualitative research provides the same type of orientation that statistics now provides for the experimental and/or quantitative researcher though these writings have not yet been organized into a subdiscipline like statistics. While the qualitative re-searcher will not have to confront statistics, the tasks of understanding and presenting qualitative research is as demanding as the task of understanding statistics.

To help you understand the methods of qualitative research we are first presenting some of the philosophical underpinnings and then providing examples and activities to 'hook' you into the research while also grounding you in the philosophy of a qualitative approach to inquiry. Our hope in placing the philosophic underpinning of a qualitative approach to inquiry within a how-to-do-it research book is that beginning qualitative researchers will see the relatedness of the philosophy to the research which they are conducting and the examples presented here. It has been our experience that beginning researchers are helped by understanding the different ways words, actions and documents are used in the opposing research paradigms.

To understand the world under investigation, people's words and actions are used by qualitative researchers. The two chapters that follow will provide a beginning methodology for the use of people's words, actions and documents within a qualitative perspective. This short introduction will not provide answers to the problem of using and understanding peoples' words in qualitative research but will provide a prologue to what follows.

Why words? Simply stated, using the subjects' words better reflects the postulates of the qualitative paradigm. The qualitative researchers looks to understanding a situation as it is constructed by the participants. The qualitative researchers attempts to capture what people say and do, that is, the products of how people interpret the world. The task for the qualitative researcher is to capture this process of interpretation. To do this requires an empathic understanding or the ability to reproduce in one's own mind the feeling, motives, and thoughts behind the actions of others (Bogden and Taylor, 1975: 13–14). Words are the way that most people come to understand their situations. We create our world with words. We explain ourselves with words. We defend and hide ourselves with words. The task of the qualitative researcher is to find patterns within those words (and actions) and to present those patterns for others to inspect while at the same time staying as close to the construction of the world as the participants originally experienced it. Bruner argues in *Actual Minds, Possible Worlds* that the examination of people's stories captures the particulars of people's lives and what they mean, while the positivist paradigm with its mathematical approach 'seeks to transcend the particular by higher and higher reaching for abstraction, and in the end disclaims in principle any explanatory values at all where the particular is concerned' (1986: 13). In other words, from the qualitative perspective, to present this situation mathematically by using statistics would be to strip the experience of its meaning, that is, the meaning as the participants experienced it.

Further, to present the results of the research to the participants in a manner which they can understand is to include the participants in the discovery. If the knower and the known are interdependent (Postulate II), then there must be integrity between how the researcher experiences the participants in the study, how the participants experience the situation and their participation in it, and how those results are presented.

Research exercise #1: Understanding the role of people's words and actions

The purpose of this exercise is to provide first-hand experience concerning the difference between a descriptive or narrative understanding of a situation and understanding the same situation statistically.

1   Write a diary entry about a classroom discussion you recently observed. Write a detailed description of a part of that discussion. When possible use quotes from the participants as best as you can remember them.
2   From your notes, count the number of times each student participated in the discussion. Make a column for student names, then another column for the number of responses by that student. Now, add the number of responses and average the total to get average responses per student.
3   Which of the two entries best fit the qualitative paradigm?

Note: The activities in the first section of the book will provide you with a sense of what qualitative research feels like, though they are *not* a model for conducting qualitative research.

Perspectival versus objective views

The importance of maintaining integrity of the subjects in the research results discussed earlier relates closely to the discussion of the perspectival versus the objective observer. Why advocate a perspectival view when an objective view is almost synonymous with good research in the minds of many persons? Why would someone want to conduct a research project which was not objective? Or, an even more serious criticism of qualitative research, why would someone attempt to make a case for a way of doing research which is not objective? Isn't a lack of objectivity synonymous with sloppy research? Look back at Postulates II and V before answering the above questions.

Word meanings can be slippery. Defining words is also a political activity. It is in part because of the political nature of word meaning that we use *perspectival* rather than *subjective*. Subjective and objective are considered opposites by many and, it would seem appropriate to compare these two words. However, the word subjective carries too much connotative baggage to help a beginning qualitative researcher understand more fully its application. The short examination of subjective and objective within the history of research provides some sense of our word choice.

The traditional position has had the advantage of defined *objective* and *subjective* as they relate to research. Therefore, objective has come to mean true, factual, and real. By default, subjective has come to mean partially-true, tentative, and less-than-real. However, one might take another look at the word objective and develop a different sense of the word. An object is a thing, an entity. An object is other; to be objective is to make something into other. To be objective is to be cold and distant. Within this framework, subjective also takes on a different meaning: to be subjective is to be aware of the agency, that is, of action. From the phenomenological point of view, subjective is synonymous with agency or with the actor's perspective. To be subjective, therefore, is to 'tend to' the subject. The speech patterns and behavior of actors or agents and the specific context in which these behaviors occur are what the qualitative researcher is trying to understand. The purpose of qualitative research is to get at the world of the agent or subject.

Further, qualitative researchers understand that they are also subjects or actors and not outside of the process as impartial observers. Subjective researchers are exposed to the same constraints in understanding the world as are the persons they are investigating. This point is exemplified in Postulate II; the world of the knower and what is to be known (the known) are one.

Understanding the way that the two practices (traditional and qualitative) use the words subjective and objective is a beginning point for the qualitative researcher. However, as the qualitative researcher knows very well, words carry meanings, even meanings that are not intended. Therefore, we have chosen to use the word perspectival instead of subjective to refer to the way qualitative researchers see the world. Perspectival has the added advantage of being inclusive of differing perspectives, including but not limited to the researchers' perspective. Without a good understanding of the different observer perspectives of the research approaches, the new qualitative researcher is likely to misunderstand the tasks of data collection and analysis which are central to all research paradigms.

Research exercise #2: Using your own experience to understand the paradigm shift

The purpose of Research Exercise #2 is to gain a better understanding of the different ways one might answer the questions raised in Postulates of the Research Paradigm (Table 2.1).

1   Look to your own experience to make a case for the qualitative orientation to research. Recall an incident from your past which would be viewed differently from another point of view. After you have articulated your story from your point

of view, rethink (rewrite) the story from the point of view of another person in the incident. Now think of what an objective view of the incident might be. Does the objective version of the story capture the story? Can there be a totally objective version of the story?

2   Now re-examine all the postulates. Your examination and reflection of the incident and the postulates should give you a better understanding of the philosophical underpinning of qualitative research.

Discovery versus proof

The goal of qualitative research is to discover patterns which emerge after close observation, careful documentation, and thoughtful analysis of the research topic. What can be discovered by qualitative research are not sweeping generalizations but contextual findings. This process of discovery is basic to the philosophic underpinning of the qualitative approach. Again Michael Polanyi shapes our understanding of this process. Discovery is understood in the relationship between what Polanyi calls the subsidiary and the focal. Polanyi argues that no knowledge is, or can be, wholly focal or, as we might say totally in focus. When trying to discover something or to uncover a problem, the subsidiary looms large because we do not know in a focal sense what we are looking for, and yet we can look because we rely on clues to its nature. It is through these clues that we somehow anticipate what we have not yet plainly understood. Further, these clues are held in subsidiary rather than focal awareness (Grene, 1969). This searching for pattern to help understand a given person, situation or phenomena is an activity for qualitative research as it is based on Postulates I (reality is multiple and constructed), IV (events are simultaneously and mutually shaped) and VI (the goal of this approach is discovery).

Isn't it also possible to make a strong case for quantitative research as a method of discovery? The answer is not obvious but can be understood by examining the nature and role of the hypothesis in quantitative research. A hypothesis is a hunch or educated guess which is set up in a particular manner so as to prove or verify something. More accurately, a null hypothesis is established so that all other alternate explanations can be eliminated. But where does the hypothesis come from? The answer is that it comes from the observation of specific people and events. Further, the hypothesis is formed when these observations coalesce into a hunch. This hunch is then refined into a hypothesis. The observation and the discernment of patterns come before the hypothesis, not after it, that is, the discovery comes before the proof. And as Bruner argues, the mathematical approach 'seeks to transcend the particular by higher and higher reaching for abstraction, and in the end disclaims in principle any explanatory values at all where the particular is concerned' (1986: 13).

Summary

Understanding the philosophic underpinnings of the two research traditions as exemplified in the postulates is, we believe, an essential beginning place for students of research. It is even more important for students who are beginning qualitative researchers since the assumptions of the qualitative traditions are not well known in the larger community. If philosophic assumptions are left unarticulated they become a stumbling block for solving research problems.

A working knowledge of the philosophic underpinnings of qualitative research is necessary even to identify a researchable problem. After a researchable problem has been identified, one has to figure out how to begin thinking through that problem. Metaphorically, unarticulated philosophical assumptions are like an unlighted room. Without the light of an articulated philosophical perspective, one is likely to stumble over objects and to misunderstand the nature of the rooms within which one is stumbling around. To extend this metaphor, turning on the light provides some help. However, research is always complex and difficult and turning on the lights (understanding the philosophical underpinnings) will provide only an opportunity to see what the problem is. To solve these research problems one needs to develop and use a set of tools. These tools are best used by persons who know what they are working on. This chapter, and to a considerable extent the next two chapters, are an effort to turn on the lights, that is, to articulate the philosophic underpinnings of qualitative research. Further, while the main purpose of the philosophic chapters is to provide a grounding in the underlying positions taken within the two research paradigms in order to guide research practices, this background should also be of assistance in defending qualitative research to colleagues as serious, rigorous and important.

Note

1 We use the word postulate to emphasize the arbitrary nature of the claim for truth. The term axiom implies worthiness and general acceptance of an idea that seems at odds with a postmodern world view.

References

AINSWORTH, M. (1979) 'Mother-infant attachment', *American Psychologist*, **34**, pp. 932–37.

BELENKY, M.F., CLINCHY, B.M., GOLDBERGER, N.R. and TARULE, J.M. (1986) *Women's Ways of Knowing: The Development of Self, Voice and Mind*, New York: Basic Books.

BOGDEN, R. and TAYLOR, S. (1975) *Introduction to Qualitative Research Methods: A Phenomenological Approach to the Social Sciences*, New York: Wiley.

BRUNER, J. (1986) *Actual Minds, Possible Worlds*, Cambridge, MA: Harvard.

CAMPBELL, D. (1975) 'Degrees of freedom', *Comparative Political Studies*, **8**, pp. 178–93.

GILLIGAN, C. (1982) *In a Different Voice: Psychological Theory and Women's Development*, Cambridge, MA: Harvard University Press.

GRENE, M. (Ed) (1969) *Knowing and Being: Essays by Michael Polanyi*, Chicago, IL: University of Chicago.

HABERMAS, J. (1989) *The Philosophical Discourse of Modernity: Twelve Lectures*, Cambridge, MA: MIT.

HEISENBERG, W. (1958) *Physics and Philosophy*, New York: Harper and Row.

HESSE, E. (1980). *The Revolution and Reconstruction of Science*, Bloomington: University of Indiana Press.

KELLER, E. (1985) *Reflections on Gender and Science*, New Haven, CJ: Yale University.

KUHN, T. (1962) *The Structure of Scientific Revolutions*, Chicago, IL: University of Chicago.

LINCOLN, Y.S. and GUBA, E.G. (1985) *Naturalistic Inquiry*, Beverly Hills, CA: Sage.

LINCOLN, Y.S. (1990) 'Campbell's retrospective and a constructionist perspective', *Harvard Educational Review*, **60**, pp. 501–04.

MAXWELL, J.A. (1990a) 'Up from positivism', *Harvard Educational Review*, **60**, pp. 497–501.

MAXWELL, J.A. (1990b) Response to 'Campbell's retrospective and a constructionist perspective', *Harvard Educational Review*, **60**, pp. 405–08.

PERRY, W.G. (1970) *Forms of Intellectual and Ethical Development in the College Years: A Scheme*, New York: Holt, Rinehart, and Winston.

O'DONOHUE, R. (1989) 'The (even) bolder model: The clinical psychologist as metaphysician–scientist–practitioner', *American Psychologist*, **44**, pp. 1460–8.

POLANYI, M. (1958) *Personal Knowledge: Toward a Post-critical Philosophy*, Chicago, IL: The University of Chicago.

ROGERS, C. (1942) 'The use of electrically recorded interviews in improving psychotherapeutic techniques', *American Journal of Orthopsychiatry*, **12**, pp. 429–34.

ROGERS, C. (1951) *Client-centered Therapy*, Cambridge, MA: Riverside.

Schwartz, P. and Ogilvy, J. (1979) *The Emerging Paradigm: Changing Patterns of Thought and Belief,* Analytic report no. 7, Values and the life style program, Menlo Park, CA: SR1 International.

Stake, R. (1978) 'The case-study in social inquiry', *Educational Researcher,* 7, pp. 5–8.

Chapter 3

The Qualitative Posture: Indwelling

A posture can be defined as a state or condition taken by one person at a given time especially in relation to other persons or things. This is the meaning of the title of this chapter: A qualitative researcher assumes the posture of indwelling while engaging in qualitative research. This posture (indwelling) is very different from the posture of a quantitative researcher because each research orientation is based on different sets of postulates regarding the nature of the world and the implication of those postulates on the conducting of research.

To indwell means to exist as an interactive spirit, force or principle, and to exist *within* as an activating spirit, force or principle. It literally means to live between, and within. Perhaps this dictionary definition can be translated for qualitative research to mean being at one with the persons under investigation, walking a mile in the other person's shoes, or understanding the person's point of view from an empathic rather than a sympathetic position. Polanyi states in *Knowing and Being*:

> To this extent knowing is an indwelling; that is a utilization of the framework for unfolding our understanding in accordance with the indications and standards imposed by the framework . . . If an act of knowing affects our choice between alternate frameworks, or modifies the framework in which we dwell, it involves a change in our way of being.
>
> (Grene, 1969: 84)

This indwelling, as the quote indicates, is also reflective. To reflect is to pause and think; to process what has gone before. The qualitative researcher is a part of the investigation as a participant observer, an in-depth interviewer, or a leader of a focus group but also removes himself from the situation to rethink the meanings of the experience.

While information gathering and interpretation of information is the task of all research, one of the fundamental differences between traditional research and qualitative research concerns the methods and tools for the collection and analysis of data. The traditional researcher attempts to be, and in fact claims to achieve, objectivity through the use of their information gathering tools such as standardized tests, and mathematical or statistical analysis. Working from a different world view (see Table 2.2), the qualitative researcher attempts to gain an understanding of a person or situation that is meaningful for those involved in the inquiry. To reach their goals, researchers in the traditional orientation look to reliable and valid non-human instruments of data collection and statistical analysis, while the qualitative inquirer looks to indwelling as a posture and to the *human-as-instrument* for the collection and analysis of data.

The human-as-instrument is a concept coined by Lincoln and Guba to illustrate the unique position taken by qualitative researchers and builds implicitly on Polanyi's concept of indwelling. A person, that is, a human-as-instrument, is the only instrument which is flexible enough to capture the complexity, subtlety, and constantly changing situation which is the human experience (1985). And it is human experiences and situations that are the subjects of qualitative research. Human-as-instrument simply means that it is the person with all of her or his skills, experience, background, and knowledge as well as biases which is the primary, if not the exclusive, source of all data collection and analysis. Lincoln and Guba argue that a human instrument is responsive, adaptable and holistic. Further, a human investigator has knowledge based experience, possesses an immediacy of the situation, and has the opportunity for clarification and summary on the spot. Finally, a human investigator can explore the atypical or idiosyncratic responses in ways that are not possible for any instrument which is constructed in advance of the beginning of the study (1985).

Traditionally oriented inquirers or quantitative researchers, on the other hand, assume the world can be broken into simpler parts and therefore observed by less complex, non-human instruments. Those who follow the tenants of the positivist position believe that a standardized instrument, a pre-designed study can capture the topic under investigation (including human behavior) because they view reality as quantifiable, as objective and as divisible into smaller and smaller parts without distorting the phenomena under investigation.

In a manner very similar to Lincoln and Guba, Michael Polanyi compares the complexity of people to simplicity of inanimate objects: 'Persons and problems are felt to be more profound, because we expect them yet to reveal themselves in unexpected ways in the future, while cobblestones evoke no such expectations' (Polanyi, 1967: 32). What people do in a given situation can never be fully predicted or predetermined. Polanyi summarizes the complexity of observing the human phenomena as follows: '. . . as we proceed to survey the ascending stages of life, our subject matter will tend to include more and more of the very faculties on which we rely for understanding it. We realize then that what we observe about the capacities of living beings must be consonant with our reliance on the same capacities for observing it' (1958: 347). In other words, the subject matter is as complex as the observer. Human situations and human beings are too complex to be captured by a static one-dimensional instrument.

If one cannot capture humans and human situations with a single instrument or a single observation, what is a researcher to do? The answer, from the point of view of the phenomenological perspective, to the question of how one finds out about the complexities of problems and persons is indwelling; the research framework which we suggest is the posture taken by a qualitative researcher, by the human-as-instrument. A qualitative researcher learns about significant aspects of reality by indwelling in these complexities. These complexities, as Lincoln and Guba state, cannot be figured out, cannot be understood by one-dimensional, reductionist approaches; they demand the human-as-instrument; they demand indwelling. To restate, the human instrument is the only data collection instrument which is multifaceted enough and complex enough to capture the important elements of a human person or activity.

Human Plurality and Indwelling

> Enter into the world. Observe and wonder; experience and reflect. To understand a world you must become part of that world while at the same time remaining separate, a part of and apart from. Go then, and return to tell me what you see and hear, what you learn, and what you come to understand.
>
> (Patton, 1980: 121)[1]

A human being can be an instrument of inquiry and thus explore idiosyncrasies and find patterns of behavior, in part, because of what Hannah Arendt in *The Human Condition* (1958) calls human plurality. Human plurality, the basic condition of both action and speech, has the twofold characteristic of equality and distinction. If we were not equal we could not understand each other or those who came before us. If we were not distinct we would not need to understand each other. Our need to understand and be understood gives rise to inserting ourselves into the world through speech and action. Arendt states that we create a 'web of meaning' and are also brought into already existing webs of meaning. These webs of meaning are the context in which we reveal ourselves to others. Equality allows for some access to the inner world of others because in some important ways we are all alike, while distinction makes it necessary for the other person to attempt to communicate through words and action what they experience internally because we are all different in other ways (Morehouse, 1991). This plurality establishes both the need for and the difficulty of communication, of understanding the speech and actions of others. Understanding communication is difficult even if the other person tells us how she feels about a situation. However, this telling does not provide direct knowledge of that person's world. The inquirer must translate the information and this translation is colored by the inner experiences and feeling of the inquirer (Schumacher, 1977).

Arendt sees action, that is, people speaking and acting in the public domain, as one of the defining characteristics of human nature[2]. She further sees action as revealing human nature. Arendt states in *On the Human Condition*: 'This revelatory quality of speech and action comes to the fore where people are with others and neither for nor against them — that is, in sheer human togetherness' (1958: 180). *Sheer human togetherness* is another way of stating, another way of understanding the posture of indwelling. In fact, it is the ability to be with others that distinguishes the qualitative researcher. When a person indwells in a situation, he or she is with the person, i.e., the qualitative researcher experiencing the world in a similar way with the participant. Thus indwelling is not arbitrary but is based on a standard of what is tacitly known of the subject or situation of the indwelling. That standard is based on human plurality.

We can indwell in a human setting, in a human activity, or with a person because of human plurality, that is, the condition of being distinct from and equal to all other humans. The human-as-instrument is connected to the topic of investigation both intentionally and philosophically. In other words, as the second postulate of the alternate paradigm states the knower and the known are connected. Importantly, the qualitative researcher recognizes this connection and works with it rather than against it. Arendt's idea of human plurality helps instruct us on how we might work with that postulate. We work with the postulate by recognizing both our equality and our uniqueness. Our understanding of our equality with other persons allows us access to their world, to their experiences. Our awareness of our difference instructs us that we cannot assume that our understanding of the situation is the same as the other person's understanding. We may be able to approximate that understanding by indwelling, but it is not given to us by human plurality, in fact, human plurality makes the approximation possible, but in no way guarantees it. Indwelling becomes the orientation, the posture that is essential to the qualitative researcher who is aware of human plurality and is using that awareness to develop their skill as a human instrument.

Since understanding of human experience is not a given, being with a person or in a situation becomes one of the ways that the human-as-instrument comes to understand the person or setting under investigation. If it is true, as Ortega taught, that we comprehend only what we see being born (Silver, 1978), then indwelling is the way qualitative researchers understand persons and situations, as indwelling allows the researcher to see things coming into existence. Indwelling requires the investment of sufficient time to learn the culture, test for misinformation introduced by distortion either of self or of respondents, and to build trust. Indwelling places the qualitative researcher in a situation long enough to understand things as they unfold. Indwelling allows the researcher to identify those elements or characteristics in the situation or person that are most relevant to the problem or issue being pursued. Further, indwelling is the posture required to focus on these persons or situations in detail. Indwelling allows the inquirer to see differences within similar situations and similarities in different situations. Indwelling is essential to qualitative research given the powers and restraints of human plurality.

Indwelling as Authentic Investigation

Go forth now. Go forth and question. Ask and listen. The world is just beginning to open up to you. Each person you question can take you into a new part of the world. For the person who is willing to ask and listen, the world will always be new. The skilled questioner and the attentive listener knows how to enter into another's experience.

(Patton, 1990: 278)[3]

How can a human instrument come to understand the world of others, their intentions, aims and purposes? What prevents the inquirer from misinterpretation of this world? Is this understanding of the world helpful to others? If so, in what ways? Again, the work of Michael Polanyi will provide a framework for building and improving the skills of the human as instrument of inquiry and provide the basis on which the trustworthiness of the naturalistic inquiry can be built. Michael Polanyi, a Hungarian born chemist, turned social scientist and philosopher of science, was drawn initially to questions of how we come to know something new because of questions concerning the politics of science. His exploration of the political nature of science led him eventually to the development of a comprehensive epistemology. His epistemology provides an answer to the question of how one acquires new knowledge.

The question 'how does one gain new knowledge' was first raised in Plato's dialogue, *The Meno*. The riddle posed in *The Meno* is as follows: Socrates engages Meno in a conversation about the nature of virtue. After dismissing several of Meno's definitions of virtue, Socrates says that he does not know the definition of virtue either, but nonetheless invites Meno to try to find the definition of virtue. Meno responds:

> Why, on what lines will you look, Socrates, for a thing of whose nature you know nothing at all? Pray, what sort of thing, amongst those that you do not know, will you treat us to as the object of your search? Or even supposing, at best, that you hit upon it, how will you know it is the thing you did not know?
>
> (Cited in Grene, 1966: 23)

This is a question which Socrates never answers; however, Polanyi in several works, provides his answer to this question (1958; 1959; 1966; Grene, 1969). Polanyi begins his answer by looking at the nature of tacit knowledge, that is, knowledge that we have but cannot state. He sees the beginning of all knowledge in tacit knowledge. '(A)ll understanding is tacit knowing, all understanding is achieved by indwelling' (Polanyi cited in Grene, 1969: 160). He says, in particular, that problems are always found, and people understood in a tacit manner.

Tacit knowledge is distinct from articulated knowledge. Tacit knowledge is what we know but cannot say. Polanyi states that tacit inquiry is like feeling one's way around in a dark cave using a stick as a probe. The inquirer's hand never touches the cave directly, yet she or he eventually learns the cave. Polanyi argues that we become aware of what is at the other end of the stick by attending away from the direct feeling in our hand and toward the meaning of the feeling. That meaning is located at the tip of the stick. We attend to the far end of the stick, not the the feeling in our hand. Thus we interpret the effect by transposing meaningless feelings into meaningful ones. This is also how we use other tools (Morehouse, 1979).

This may appear to be a long way to go to understand tacit knowledge, but the stick or probe in a dark cave is a good metaphor for tacit knowledge. Just as we cannot see (or perhaps say aloud what the cave looks like), we nonetheless know the cave well enough to move around in it with the help of our probe. Qualitative inquiry begins with what we know but cannot say, it begins with tacit knowledge.

Tacit knowledge

Two types of knowledge play a part in the way we understand the world, tacit and explicit knowledge, but tacit knowledge is more basic — it comes before explicit knowledge. Tacit knowledge is unarticulated knowledge; it is unformulated, such as the type of knowledge we have in the act of doing something. Explicit knowledge is that which is or can be written down in words, maps, or mathematical formulas. The major logical difference between the two types of knowledge is that explicit knowledge can be subject to critical reflection, while tacit knowledge cannot be reflected on. What this means in practice is that as we begin a qualitative research project we will rely on our tacit knowledge as well as our explicit knowledge in order to understand the situation. Our explicit knowledge can be entered into our field notes, while our tacit knowledge will aid us in understanding the environment 'by the seat of our pants'. As we articulate our observations, reflect on what we know explicitly, we will begin to uncover our tacit knowledge. Once this tacit knowledge is made explicit, it too can be reflected on. As Michael Polanyi states, 'But articulation does not merely make us better informed: it enriches us more by increasing our mental power over the given piece of information' (1959: 24).

Tacit knowledge is gained by indwelling. When one lives within a situation one learns to pay attention to the subsidiary, that is, one learns to attend away from the object and toward the meaning of the object. This is what we do in reading, for example. In order to read this passage, you must focus away from the letters and even the words, toward the meaning of the passage. But how do we understand problems, the actions of persons, or the meaning of institutions or rituals? Polanyi's answer is by indwelling. 'Tacit knowing now appears as an act of indwelling by which we gain access to a new meaning. When exercising a skill we literally dwell in the innumerable muscular acts which contribute to its purpose, a purpose which constitutes their joint meaning' (Polanyi in Grene, 1969: 160).

What becomes known by indwelling is not just the pieces, but the whole — what Polanyi calls *joint meaning*. It is 'not by looking at things, but by indwelling in them, that we understand their joint meaning' (Polanyi, 1967: 18). By attending away from or perhaps through the pieces to the meaning of the pieces is the way we understand the whole. This is the paradox of tacit knowledge and of indwelling: The pieces of the puzzle are essential to knowing the whole, but in order to gain an understanding of the whole, we must experience, rather than attend to, these pieces, thus allowing the whole to emerge from the experience. Tacit knowledge dwells in our awareness of particulars while bearing on an entity which the particulars jointly constitute. In order to share this indwelling, the qualitative researcher must presume that the activity of the participants in the study which appears at the moment to be meaningless will, in fact, become meaningful as the researcher participates alongside these participants (Polanyi, 1967). Understanding occurs in this tacit manner: We can only understand problems, institutions and persons in this same indirect way. In effect, we understand the trees as they are a subsidiary part of the forest. Understanding of persons is gained to the extent to which we can dwell in the external workings of their minds from outside. According to Marjorie Grene, who edits a collection of Polanyi's writings entitled *Knowing and Being: Essays by Michael Polanyi*, we can do this fairly well since many tacit functions of our mind are accessible by attending to behavior (1969).

In understanding tacit and explicit knowledge, that is, in understanding the *modus operandi* of a naturalistic inquirer, it is helpful to know more about the relationship between the thing to be known and the knower. A person has access to knowledge because of a three-way relationship between the subsidiary, the focal and the knower, according to Michael Polanyi. A person sees the world which is mostly background or subsidiary. In order to bring an object into the foreground (focal), a person focuses attention. While focusing attention, the person remains a part of the world which he or she is observing. The knower controls what is ground and what is figural, what is subsidiary and what is focal, but cannot stand outside of the situation being observed. Marjorie Grene (1969) in summarizing Polanyi's ideas about the effects of subsidiary awareness on problem-solving, outlines his central thesis: no knowledge is, or can be *wholly* focal. Polanyi develops his argument by examining how problems are identified and solved. He sees problems as a special case that helps in understanding tacit and focal knowledge. For with problems, the subsidiary aspect looms even larger. One of the paradoxes of problem finding is that in a focal sense, we do not know what we are looking for when we are looking for a problem. How is this possible? It is possible, paradoxically, because in looking for this problem, we rely on clues to its nature, clues which are in the background or subsidiary. These clues somehow allow us to anticipate what we have not yet plainly understood. These unnamed, perhaps unnameable clues we hold in subsidiary rather than focal awareness (Grene, 1969). Any type of trouble-shooting provides a commonplace example. If one has a problem with an automobile or a washing machine, one does not know the nature of the problem initially. One only knows that the machine does not work. However, many clues are available. By looking to one clue, examining its consequences, then looking to the next clue, one quickly or eventually arrives at the problem which is responsible for the malfunction.

To place Polanyi's central thesis into the activity of doing naturalistic inquiry, or qualitative research, what the searcher is looking for cannot be seen directly; it appears in the shadows. (The way qualitative researchers ask initial research questions is embedded in this orientation and will be explored in the next chapter.) The patterns which will explain the phenomena under investigation emerge from the data as shapes begin to form in the background. These patterns are formed within the context of the situation observed. In order to understand a person or a phenomenon, one needs to understand the context that surrounds the person or phenomenon. The naturalist inquirer does not know directly what he is looking for at the beginning of a research project because he does not know the context. One can further state that for the qualitative researcher, the person or the event can only be understood within the context or background. The person that emerges out of the context is not a universal person or event but rather a contextual person or event.

However, by immersing oneself in the situation, and by looking for general clues, shapes and forms, the naturalistic inquirer can anticipate what is yet not plainly understood. These clues are on the edges of the investigator's awareness. Through this process of looking at the background, patterns begin to take shape; in Polanyi's language, these things become focal. This focal knowledge can be further intensified through articulation. The ongoing descriptive reports (such as field notes) have their value in part because they are the means by which the inquirer makes the implicit (the subsidiary) explicit (articulate). Articulated information increases our ability to understand what we observe and also aids our ability to use our tacit knowledge. Polanyi sees all knowing based in tacit understanding. We know more than we can say, and the more we can say, the more our unarticulated or tacit knowledge grows.

Research exercise #3: Understanding tacit and explicit knowledge

This research exercise is intended to help you understand how you use tacit knowledge in your everyday effort at understanding the world around you. Further, you will better understand the role of making tacit knowledge explicit in extending your understanding. You will need pencil and paper for this activity.

1 Pick a sports activity or any other physical activity that you do with some regularity. Do that activity. Can you explain how you did it?
2 Now observe someone else doing that same activity. Write down what you observe in as straightforward a manner as possible. Now reflect on your doing of this activity. Do you have a more complete sense of the complexity of that activity? If you do, you have moved your understanding of that activity from tacit to explicit.

Tolerance for ambiguity

Achieving understanding (the goal of qualitative inquiry) is not an easy task; it depends in part on the personal quality of tolerance for ambiguity. In many ways, the task of the traditional researcher is easier. The traditionalist sets out to narrow the subject of inquiry before the investigation begins. He or she posits one or more hypotheses which focus the inquiry and which tell the researcher what to exclude from the study. The task of the qualitative inquirer is more ambiguous. Maurice Merleau-Ponty discusses this process in an essay entitled 'Cézanne's Doubt'. He outlines the difficulty of the qualitative researcher using the painter Paul Cézanne as a prototypic phenomenologist, or as we would say, a qualitative inquirer:

> His painting was paradoxical: he was pursuing reality without giving up the sensuous surface, with no other guide than the immediate impression of nature, without following contours, with no outline to enclose the colors, with no perspectival or pictorial arrangement.
>
> (Merleau-Ponty, 1964: 12)

It is particularly the sensuous surfaces that the qualitative inquirer explores. He or she does so by following the contours of the investigations as they emerge, that is, not as a pre-set research script to follow in detail. The task of the naturalistic inquirer is to capture what people say and do as indicators of how people interpret their world (Bogden and Taylor, 1975). The perspective of the qualitative researcher is, therefore, open-ended and not clearly focused in its initial stages. The pictorial arrangement (that is, the key pieces of information in the study) change their meaning as new information comes into play and new perspectives are discovered.

To understand the data as it unfolds, that is, to find patterns within the data, a naturalistic researcher must have patience and accept tentative patterns and must possess a willingness to give up or to reconstruct these tentative patterns. To refer back to the quote about Cezanne's approach to painting, the naturalistic inquirer must continue to be guided by the sensuous surface, must move toward letting the painting establish its own contours, while constantly looking for the patterns as they emerge from the study. It is an extremely difficult task to 'let the data speak for itself'. It requires a tolerance for ambiguity.

A short definitional aside may be in order here. Ambiguity and vagueness are terms often used interchangeably; however, these words have different meanings which might aid in understanding a tolerance for ambiguity. An ambiguous situation is one which can be understood in more than one way. A vague situation, on the other hand, is one which lacks precision. While a qualitative researcher will need tolerance for both vagueness and ambiguity, these tolerances are of a slightly different sort. One can resolve a vague understanding by getting more exact information. For example, if the temperature is cool, one can find the exact degrees centigrade and the word cool will no longer be vague. However, if I say, 'it's cool', the listener needs to know what I am referring to, that is, the temperature outside, or a person. Knowing the degrees centigrade, that is, making things more specific, may not be helpful as *cool* may mean several different things in a given situation. A qualitative researcher's need to find more precise information (and tolerance is required in that process as the information may become more precise within the situation under observation) to resolve a vague situation. Perhaps, a more important quality in a qualitative researcher is tolerance for ambiguity; the ability to hold two or more different interpretations of an event, activity or person in mind, while waiting to see which interpretation is merited by the data which you are in the process of collecting.

Often, the inner world of others is initially seen as ambiguous. One of the ways these inner worlds can be made less ambiguous, or, to put it more positively, can be comprehended in all their ambiguity, is through stories. These stories unfold over time and the meaning of one event is understood in terms of both what came before it as well as what comes after it. Arendt's words, 'webs of meaning', gets at this complex interweaving of events. Arendt states that we insert ourselves into the world, into these webs of meaning which we call stories. Stories reveal an agent, that is, they reveal a person as an actor. Arendt, in a further exploration of speech and action, states that the speaker reveals himself only to the other in 'a backward glance'. This means that the listener may understand the story of the teller or actor more fully than does the person telling or creating the story (Arendt, 1958).

Research exercise #4:   Working with ambiguity

This research exercise is intended to help understand the ambiguous nature of an unfolding experience by using a short story as your field experience. Camus' (1957) 'Artist at work' is a workable example.

1   Read the first 15 pages or so and make some notes as to the salient features of the lead characters, the setting, and the direction of the story line. Put these notes aside as you read the next 10 or 15 pages.
2   Again, write some notes on the salient aspect of these 15 or so pages. Now go back and read your initial notes. Compare your notes on the first 15 pages. Are their some ambiguities? In other words, are some of your observations about the initial characteristics of the setting, the story line or the lead actors different from your reading of the first 15 pages? If they are you have experienced ambiguity. These conflicting perspectives or understandings cannot be resolved without further reading. To keep these conflicting understandings in mind — in the air, so to speak — is to tolerate ambiguity.
3   Continue reading the rest of the story in the same manner. At the end of the story, while an undisputed interpretation may not emerge, you will be able to resolve many of the ambiguous interpretations regarding character, story line and setting.
4   An alternate way to gain some sense of the importance of a tolerance for ambiguity is to reconstruct your understanding of a short story or novel which you enjoyed but struggled to understand. Reconstruct your struggle in roughly the same steps outlined above.

It is this backward glance that provides the beginning place for understanding the world of appearances and intentions. And it is understanding of people as agents or actors that the naturalistic inquirer is seeking. Van Wright defines understanding, as opposed to other forms of knowing, as connected to the aims and purposes of agents; it is connected to intentions (1971). Bogdan and Taylor in their book, *Introduction to Qualitative Research Methods*, extend this point by stating, 'The qualitative researcher views human behavior — what people say and do — as products of how people interpret their world' (1975: 13). They go on to say the the qualitative inquirer seeks to capture the *process* of interpretation (p. 14).

Meno's question

How has the following examination of tacit knowledge and tolerance for ambiguity addressed Meno's question? To place Meno's question within the context of qualitative research: Can the qualitative researcher capture the process of interpretation? Can the qualitative researcher understand agents and their intentions? The answer, stated as directly as possible, is this: By understanding the connection between tacit knowledge and human plurality (equality and distinctiveness allow tacit access to individuals and human situations) and by maintaining a tolerance for ambiguity (avoiding premature closure on the subject under investigation), the researcher comes to understand the phenomena as patterns emerge. These patterns are recognized as valid as they are consonant with our own experiences, and yet we recognize the unique qualities of the persons or situations under investigation. We can feel confident, though not certain, if we have dwelled within the situation and observed closely what emerges from it. Again, to paraphrase Arendt: if we were not equal we could not possibly understand others, if we were not distinct, we would not need communication beyond points and grunts. The qualitative researchers develop their human skills of observing, questioning and probing to gain a more accurate picture of the world of others.

Narrativity

Mikhail Bakhtin (1986) in his note fragments collected under the title 'Toward a methodology for the human sciences' goes to the heart of qualitative research, that is, the connection between the knower and the known. To state Bakhtin's point: If a person (or subject as he says) is to be understood as a person and not as a thing, then the relationship between the researcher and the other person must be a dynamic and mutual relationship, what he calls a dialogue. He sees the researcher and the subject of the research connected as in a dialogue or interchange with one affecting the other. Postulate II of the qualitative paradigm (See Table 2.1) states: The knower and the known are interdependent. The knower cannot stand outside of what is to be known. Bakhtin's understanding of human subjectivity as it applies to qualitative research points to the connectedness and the interaction between knower and known within a narrative.

A narrative, according to Jerome Bruner in *Actual Minds, Possible Worlds* (1986) and *Acts of Meaning* (1990) deals with the vicissitudes or changing nature of intentions. Intentions include beliefs, desires and commitment. Intentions are central to understanding an agent or an actor, that is, understanding a participant in a qualitative study. Qualitative research examines persons as agents. Bruner defines an agent as one who acts on intentional states such as beliefs, desires and commitments, states which are in fluctuation (1990).

As meaning is central to qualitative research, our use of the word needs some explanation. Meaning is what we can agree upon or at least accept as a working basis for seeking agreement about a concept at hand. We achieve meaning through shared encounters. Bruner argues in *Acts of Meaning* that meaning-making is embedded within narrative or stories (1990). Our stories are lived experiences to which we, in concert with others, give meaning to those experiences. The qualitative researcher can examine the meanings of these stories because they are public and shared. Meaning, contrary to the beliefs of the traditional paradigm (as epitomized by the behaviorist in psychology) is neither hidden nor private. These meanings may be complex and multidimensional, but they are public and shared otherwise we would not be able to understand one another. These constructed meanings are possible because of what Hannah Arendt calls human plurality, that is, we are both distinct (that is, unique) and equal (Arendt, 1958). Given the qualitative researcher's immersion in culture, qualitative research must be organized around those meaning-making activities that connect a person to a culture.

Summary

As a way of summarizing as well as providing an additional tool for looking at the role of the human-as-instrument, it might be helpful to think about qualitative research as the 'reading' of a situation. Robert Scholes develops an approach to understanding or interpretation of a text, persons and events in his *Protocols of Reading*, which while focusing on the process of reading and writing, is very similar to the ideas discussed above. Scholes first explores the idea that reading a text or a situation might be understood metaphorically as a process of looking both forward and backwards (1989). The process of naturalistic inquiry looks back to events to be observed in order to clearly describe the events as they were unfolding and looks forward to the meaning which these events might have in the lived experience of the participants. Scholes then goes on to explore and reject this metaphor as well as another metaphor for understanding reading a text, or interpreting a situation, that of centripetal and centrifugal force, or a closing and opening of a circle. The issue here is what pulls things together and what pulls things apart or what should be included within the circle, and what should be placed outside it. This metaphor is rejected as helpful but not accurate enough to uncover the meaning of a text, or a person, or an event. As each metaphor is explored and abandoned in turn, Scholes uses the idea of the construction and abandonment of metaphors itself as a method for understanding the creative process of reading a situation. Scholes says that reading may best be thought of as forming and rejecting metaphors. All interpretation of human situations (extending Scholes, ideas on reading) is dialectical, and accepting and rejecting metaphor are a part of that dialogue (Scholes, 1989).

In naturalistic inquiry, the searcher must go back and forth between the observed situation and its meaning, as experienced by the participants and as grasped metaphorically. Meaning is not given in the situation, but emerges from the situation built on both observation and the researcher. To accomplish the task of interpretation or reading, therefore, requires both creative and critical skills. This process requires us to get as close to the thing to be understood as possible, to indwell in the thing, and to reflect on it critically and creatively.

The ideas of Scholes concerning reader situations can be seen as applications of Polanyi's ideas of the central role of tacit knowledge. Scholes is presenting a literary way of indwelling. 'It brings home to us that it is not by looking at things, but by indwelling in them, that we understand their joint meaning' (Polanyi, 1967: 18). This statement by Polanyi about indwelling might well have been made by Scholes about reading and writing. Scholes argues that reading and writing are two ends of the same process. This is similar to the way Polanyi writes about the creative and critical elements of indwelling.

Polanyi, like Scholes, believes that meaning, whether in the world or in a text, is not singular, rather meaning derives from relationships. Meaning is both joint (that is, arises from relationships) and multiple (that is, it is understood from discrete points of view within relationships). The human-as-instrument is the most appropriate way to access these meanings since the human instrument, unlike objective instruments within the positivist paradigm, which can only capture the joint and multiple meanings of human experiences.

In summary, the method of qualitative inquiry using the human-as-instrument is possible within a posture of indwelling. It is descriptive, and its objective is to identify or define a situation. Qualitative research requires mediative or reflective thinking rather than calculative thinking. It is based on a posture toward knowledge which is inclusive and indwelling, rather than exclusive and distancing. The human-as-instrument, like all ways of knowing according to Polanyi, builds on tacit knowledge. The posture of the qualitative researcher is indwelling.

Notes

1   This quote is attributed to *Halcolm's Epistemological Parables*. Halcolm is a character invented by Michael Patton to provide words of wisdom to beginning qualitative researchers.

2 The other two conditions of human life are labor, that is, what we do to get food and shelter, and work, that is, what we do to create things that live after we die.

3 This quote Patton attributes to *Halcolm's Epistemological Parables.*

References

ARENDT, H. (1958) *The Human Condition*, Chicago, IL: The University of Chicago.

BAKHTIN, M. (1986) *Speech Genres and Other Late Essays*, Translated. McGEE,V. Austin, TX: University of Texas.

BOGDAN, R. and BIKLEN, S.K. (1982) *Qualitative Research for Education*, Boston, MA: Allyn and Bacon.

BOGDAN, R. and TAYLOR, S. (1975) *Introduction to Qualitative Research Methods*, New York: Wiley.

BRUNER, J. (1990) *Acts of Meaning*, Cambridge, MA: Harvard.

BRUNER, J. (1986) *Actual Minds, Possible Worlds*, Cambridge, MA: Harvard.

CAMUS, A. (1957) *The Artist at Work in Exile and the Kingdom*, translated by O'BRIEN, J. New York: Alfred A. Knopf.

GRENE, M. (Ed) (1969) *Knowing and Being: Essays by Michael Polanyi*, Chicago, IL: University of Chicago.

GRENE, M. (1966) *The Knower and the Known*, New York, NY: Basic.

LINCOLN, Y.S. and GUBA, E.G. (1985) *Naturalistic Inquiry*, Beverly Hills, CA: Sage.

MERLEAU-PONTY, M. (1964) *Sense and Non-sense (Sens et non-sens* originally published by Nagel, 1948 translated by DREYFUS, H. and DREYFUS, P.*)* Evanston, IL: Northwestern University.

MOREHOUSE, R. (1979) *Implementor/observer: The Development and Implementation of a Conceptual Tool for Phenomenological Inquiry*, Dissertation Abstracts International (University Microfilms).

MOREHOUSE, R. (1991) 'Conversation and community', in REED, R. (Ed) *When We Talk: Essays on Classroom Conversation*, Worth Worth, TX: Analytic Teaching.

PATTON, M.Q. (1980) *Qualitative Evaluation Methods*, Beverly Hills, CA: Sage.

PATTON, M.Q. (1990) *Qualitative Evaluation Methods* (2nd Ed), Beverly Hills, CA: Sage.

POLANYI, M. (1958) *Personal Knowledge: Toward a Post-critical Philosophy*, Chicago, IL: The University of Chicago.

POLANYI, M. (1959) *The Study of Man*, Chicago, IL: The University of Chicago.

POLANYI, M. (1967) *The Tacit Dimension*, Chicago, IL: The University of Chicago.

SCHOLES, R. (1989) *Protocols of Reading*, New Haven, CT: Yale.

SCHUMACHER, E.F. (1977) *A Guide for the Perplexed*, New York: Harper and Row.

SILVER, P. (1978) *Ortega as Phenomenologist: The Genesis of Meditations on Quixote*, New York: Columbia University.

VAN WRIGHT, G. (1971) *Explanation and Understanding*, London: Routledge and Kegan Paul.

Part II

From Ideas to Outcomes: Conducting Qualitative Research

Chapter 4

Designing Qualitative Research: An Overview

The questions we ask will always to some degree determine the answers we find. This point is important in designing a qualitative study. The research questions that guide a qualitative study reflect the researcher's goal of discovering what is important to know about some topic of interest. A qualitative study has a focus but that focus is initially broad and open-ended, allowing for important meanings to be discovered.

The philosophical underpinnings of a qualitative research approach direct us to several key features that characterize this kind of research. The first three chapters were intended to place research practice within a theoretical framework. This chapter begins a hands-on application of qualitative research methodology which leads directly from the earlier presented theoretical framework. We assume that readers are seriously interested in learning about qualitative methodology so that they can critically read the qualitative research literature and conduct their own research investigations. Throughout the following chapters we continue our use of research exercises aimed at helping readers hone their skills as qualitative researchers. While it is conceivable that someone might read this book 'armchair fashion', it will be more instructive if readers actively engage in the research exercises or use the book to guide them through an actual research project.

Characteristics of Qualitative Research

Whether one is examining the literature for qualitative studies or beginning the outlines of one's own study, these eight characteristics of qualitative research are important to consider:

1 An exploratory and descriptive focus

Research studies that are qualitative are designed to discover what can be learned about some phenomenon of interest, particularly social phenomena where people are the participants (or as traditionally referred to — *subjects*). Qualitative researchers develop a general 'focus of inquiry' that helps to guide the discovery of what is to be known about some social phenomenon (Lincoln and Guba, 1985). Researchers are interested in investigating and responding to exploratory and descriptive questions such as 'What is young children's conception of "mind"?' 'In what ways do people in this rural town build informal social networks?' 'How do people who work in this place think the physical environment could be improved?' The outcome of any of these studies is not the generalization of results, but a deeper understanding of experience from the perspectives of the participants selected for study. Mary Belenky and her associates have chosen the term *interpretive-descriptive research* to refer to exploratory studies which rely on people's words and meanings as the data for analysis (Belenky, 1992). Their work on exploring women's epistemology exemplifies the rich possibilities of research investigations that are conducted from a discovery mode (Belenky, Clinchy, Goldberger and Tarule, 1986).

2 Emergent design

For students and researchers well schooled in traditional approaches to research design, the idea of a design evolving over time is contrary, and perhaps even blasphemous. Any student or researcher can, however, appreciate the experience of carrying out one's research study and discovering a feature for which one's research design did not allow consideration. It is this very notion of pursuing important or salient early discoveries that undergirds qualitative approaches to inquiry (Lincoln and Guba, 1985; Stake, 1975). Important leads are identified in the early phases of data analysis and pursued by asking new questions, observing new situations or previous situations with a slightly different lens, or examining previously unimportant documents. This broadening or narrowing of what is important to study (i.e., the focus of inquiry) and the consequent sampling of new people and settings is anticipated and planned for, as best one can, in qualitative research designs. It is possible, however, to employ a nonemergent research design, where researcher's focus of inquiry is pursued using qualitative methods of data collection and data analysis, but the data is collected, *then* analyzed. This latter form of qualitative research, while less open and responsive, has yielded important findings (see, for example, Hodgson, 1984; Melman, 1987; Saljo, 1984).

3 A purposive sample

In qualitative research, participants (or settings, such as schools or organizations) are carefully selected for inclusion, based on the possibility that each participant (or setting) will expand the variability of the sample. Purposive sampling increases the likelihood that variability common in any social phenomenon will be represented in the data, in contrast to random sampling which tries to achieve variation through the use of random selection and large sample size. For example, if we were interested in understanding how people in rural areas develop social support networks, we would probably want to include people who had social networks made up of mostly family *and* people who had networks made up of mostly friends, since the process of building social networks is likely to be different for these individuals (Maykut and Garber, 1981). As our study of rural social networks proceeded, it would become more clear who would need to be included on purpose to fully understand the development of social support networks. Thus, in an emergent research design the composition of the sample itself evolves over the course of the study.

4 Data collection in the natural setting

Qualitative researchers are interested in understanding people's experience in context. The natural setting is the place where the researcher is most likely to discover, or uncover, what is to be known about the phenomenon of interest. This characteristic of qualitative research again reflects the philosophic underpinnings of the alternate paradigm (see Table 2.1). Personal meaning is tied to context. For example, to understand more about college students' experience of academic life, the researcher goes to the classrooms, the library, the dorms or apartments, the student union, etc. to observe, to interview, to indwell. Chang (1992) provides a useful example of data collection in the natural setting, in his recent study of life in a US high school. Similarly, to explore how parents go about informally teaching their children, one goes to the places where this might happen, such as family homes, shopping centers, the YMCA, social events, etc. Extended amounts of time with people in the places they inhabit is a critical feature of indwelling, fostering the development of both explicit and tacit knowledge.

5 Emphasis on 'human-as-instrument'

We draw attention again to the key role of the researcher or the research team in the qualitative research process. While researchers are certainly pivotal in more traditional research approaches, the qualitative researcher has the added responsibility of being both the collector of relevant data — data whose relevance changes as the study proceeds — and the culler of meaning from that data, which most often is in the form of people's words and actions. It is possible to include other formal instruments, such as questionnaires or tests, in a qualitative study. In keeping with the alternative paradigm, however, instrumentation should be grounded in the data, inductively drawn from what is becoming salient to the researcher from the data she or he has already collected.

6 Qualitative methods of data collection

The data of qualitative inquiry is most often people's words and actions, and thus requires methods that allow the researcher to capture language and behavior. The most useful ways of gathering these forms of data are participant observation, in-depth interviews, group interviews, and the collection of relevant documents. Observation and interview data is collected by the researcher in the form of field notes and audio-taped interviews, which are later transcribed for use in data analysis. There is also some qualitative research being done with photographs and video-taped observations as primary sources of data (see, for example, Erickson and Wilson, 1982; Wagner, 1979).

7 Early and ongoing inductive data analysis

The characteristics of qualitative research described so far point to two important characteristics of qualitative data analysis: (a) it is an ongoing research activity, in contrast to an end stage, when the design is emergent; (b) it is primarily inductive. Analysis begins when one has accumulated a subset of the data, providing an opportunity for the salient aspects of the phenomenon under study to begin to emerge. These initial leads are followed by pursuing the relevant persons, settings, or documents that will help illuminate the phenomenon of interest. In other words, there is a broadening or narrowing of the focus of inquiry as the data suggest it. *What is important is not predetermined by the researcher.* Within the broad boundaries of the researcher's focus of inquiry, the data are studied for what is meaningful to the participants in the study, or what Bogdan and Biklen (1982) refer to as 'participant perspectives'. The outcomes of the research study evolve from the systematic building of homogeneous categories of meaning inductively derived from the data.

8 A case study approach to reporting research outcomes

The results of a qualitative research study are most effectively presented within a rich narrative, sometimes referred to as a case study.[1] The number of cases varies with each study, from one case to several. With book length reports, the researcher has an opportunity to provide many excerpts from the actual data that let the participants speak for themselves — in word or action — thereby giving the reader sufficient information for understanding the research outcomes. In article length reports, the researcher by necessity is more brief, using a modified case-study mode of reporting. A qualitative research report characterized by rich description should provide the reader with enough information to determine whether the findings of the study possibly apply to other people or settings.

Taken together, these eight features of qualitative research reflect the alternate paradigm and reinforce the connection between this paradigm and the doing of research. In addition, these eight features provide a framework for designing and implementing a qualitative research study (see Figure 4.1) . In the following chapters, we will explore each of these eight features in further detail, inviting you to engage in a series of research exercises to develop and refine your qualitative research skills.

Note

1 We are aware that the term *case study* may connote distance between the researcher and the people or settings that are the focus of the study, such as when an individual is described as a *case*. We use the term to emphasize the detailed narrative that characterizes a case-study report.

Figure 4.1:   Characteristics of qualitative research

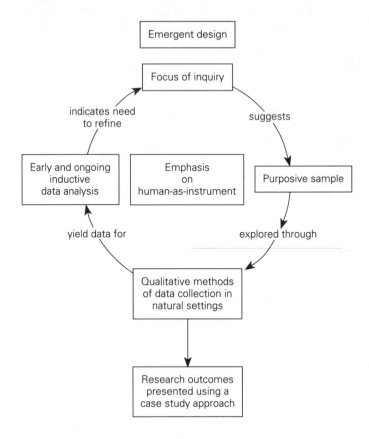

Liberally adapted from Lincoln and Guba (1985).

References

BELENKY, M.F. (1992, October) *Bringing Balance to the Classroom or Workplace*, paper presented at the Wisconsin Women's Studies Conference, Preconference Workshop, Green Bay, WI.

BELENKY, M.F., CLINCHY, B.M., GOLDBERGER, N.R. and TARULE, J.M. (1986) *Women's Ways of Knowing: The Development of Self, Voice and Mind*, New York: Basic Books.

BOGDAN, R. and BIKLEN, S.K. (1982) *Qualitative Research for Education*, Boston, MA: Allyn and Bacon.

CHANG, H. (1992) *Adolescent Life and Ethos: An Ethnography of a US High School*, London: Falmer Press.

ERICKSON, F. and WILSON, J. (1982) *Sights and Sounds of Life in Schools: A Resource Guide to Film and Videotape for Research and Education*, East

Lansing, MI: Institute for Research on Teaching, College of Education, Michigan State University.

HODGSON, V. (1984) 'Learning from lectures', in MARTON, F. HOUNSELL, D. and ENTWISTLE, N. (Eds) *The Experience of Learning*, Edinburgh: Scottish Academic Press, pp. 90–102.

LINCOLN, Y. and GUBA, E. (1985) *Naturalistic Inquiry*, Beverly Hills, CA: Sage.

MAYKUT, P.S. and GARBER, H.G. (1981) *Family and Friends: A Social Network Research Instrument*, University of Wisconsin-Madison, WI: Rehabilitation Research and Training Center.

MELMAN, L.S. (1987) 'Diabetes as experienced by adolescents', *Adolescence*, **86**, pp. 433–44.

SALJO, R. (1984) 'Learning from reading', in MARTON, F. HOUNSELL, D. and ENTWISTLE, N. (Eds) *The Experience of Learning*, Edinburgh: Scottish Academic Press, pp. 71–89.

STAKE, R.E. (Ed) (1975) *Evaluating the Arts in Education: A Responsive Approach*, Columbus, OH: Merrill.

WAGNER, J. (Ed) (1979) *Images of Information*, Beverly Hills, CA: Sage.

Chapter 5

Generating Ideas

After Lincoln and Guba (1985), we have adopted the term *focus of inquiry* to describe the initial topic that a qualitative researcher pursues. How do you generate a focus of inquiry? If you are a researcher with a topic at hand this is not a difficult task, although the fit between the qualitative research paradigm and the research question can present problems which we will discuss later. As a student in search of a research topic, developing a focus of inquiry can be quite challenging. In our work with beginning student researchers we have used the following exercise, which involves both brainstorming and concept-mapping, in order to help them arrive at a focus of inquiry.

Research exercise #5: Developing a focus of inquiry

In order to do this exercise you will need a plain blank surface to write on, such as a large sheet of typing paper. It is useful to have a few different colored markers handy for recording ideas and indicating emphasis. We have found it useful to tape large pieces of easel paper on the wall to stand at and write on for the exercise.

1   Think quietly for a few minutes about some things that interest you and that you would like to know more about. What are some things that you would like to gather more information on in order to reach a clearer understanding? Jot down these topics in a corner of your paper.
2   Select one of the topics for this exercise, perhaps the one that interests you the most. Write that topic in the center of your paper and circle it. Use the same colored marker for this and the rest of the initial brainstorming.
3   For the next 5 minutes, write down the topics and ideas that relate to the topic in the center, drawing lines from the center to each new idea, and connecting or clustering similar ideas. Do not censor yourself. Write down all the things that come to mind that relate to this topic, including questions, concerns, words and even graphic images that might come to mind that you can quickly record. Stop writing after 5 minutes.
4   Step back and reflect on your concept map. Notice what kinds of things are on your mind. Do you see any patterns to your thinking? For example, do you notice that you keep coming back to a certain phenomenon or problem, age group, gender, type of person, type of organization, etc.? Or are your ideas quite varied? Take another colored marker and connect related ideas, if you see any connections.
5   Take yet another colored marker and circle the idea that is the most intriguing to you at this time. Use this idea as the basis for your work in the following sections.

We have used this exercise ourselves and with our students in an effort to tap into our own and their creativity, as well as to converge on a topic of interest. A few of the concept maps created by students are shown in Figure 5.1.

Once a topic of interest has been identified, the next step is to develop a researchable question based on the topic, one that reflects the goals of exploration and description. Our experience indicates that this aspect of research development, while appearing simple, is fraught with difficulty for the majority of us who have been weaned on the traditional scientific method. The most frequent types of researchable questions that are initially offered by beginning researchers are often those that involve quantification and the search for causal linkages, such as:

'What are the effects of television viewing on children's prosocial behavior?'

'Which therapy approach is more beneficial in the treatment of depression, behavior therapy or insight-based psychotherapy?'

'What is the relationship between expanding gender roles and self-esteem among women?'

'Do children from single-parent families experience more school failure than children from two-parent families?'

Figure 5.1: Concept maps created by student researchers

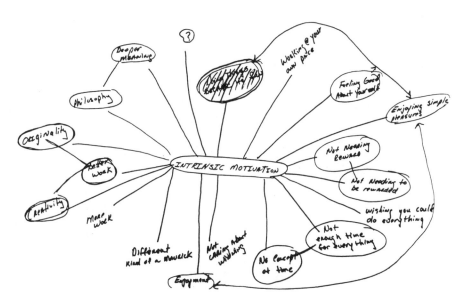

51

Figure 5.1: (Continued)

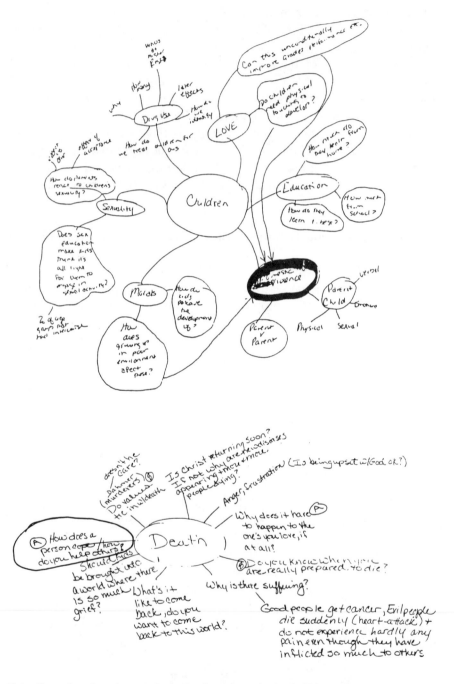

Note: Examples of student work appear throughout the book. This work is at times not completely legible, but we think these examples serve an important illustrative purpose.

These research questions would provide a useful first step to the development of hypotheses, which are the core of the traditional scientific method. They provide the basis for carrying out a study that will confirm or disconfirm a hypothesis and allow for future prediction. We are interested, however, in adopting a qualitative posture that is one of discovery and description, in an effort to gain a deeper understanding of personal and social phenomena. We believe that the difficulty in posing a qualitative research question on any topic is a function of the embeddedness of the traditional paradigm in our culture.

To Lincoln and Guba (1985) this dilemma is a matter of *paradigm fit* in the development of a focus of inquiry. In our experience there is frequently a mismatch between the types of researchable questions students initially ask and the alternative paradigm, even after careful study of the postulates (see Table 2.1). The postulates undergirding the alternative paradigm draw our attention to the phenomenology of human experience; reality is variously constructed by each of us, and we bring our multiple meanings to each act and interaction. As a result, most human phenomena are the result of multiple causes, which often escape inquiry by traditional scientific methods. Thus, while we have all probably generated qualitative research questions, questions that focus on what can be explored and what can be described, these questions have not usually been identified as or considered real research.

Developing a qualitative research question or statement frequently acts as a key to the paradigm shift necessary to conduct qualitative research. This is at times an 'aha' experience for individuals beginning qualitative research, although from the outside it seems quite simple. Once researchers select a focus of inquiry, we have found that by using the sentence stems 'I would like to know about . . .' or 'I would like to understand more about . . .' they can reformulate their topics into a research statement that is a match with the qualitative paradigm. The research questions provided above can be reformulated in the following way:

'I would like to know whether and how children take prosocial messages from television programs and make them their own.'
'I would like to understand clients' experience of insight-based psychotherapy.'
'I would like to know more about women's experience of expanding gender roles and how they evaluate themselves: Are women experiencing broader, less stereotypical social roles? Are women with expanding gender roles experiencing high levels of self-esteem, evaluating themselves positively?'

'I would like to know more about what it is like growing up in a single-parent household.'

Here are some additional examples:

'I would like to know more about college students' experience of learning from lectures.'

'I would like to understand more about interpersonal attraction among young adult men and women.'

'I would like to understand more about the perceived reasons for the high turnover of nurses in large hospitals.'

'I would like to know more about children's perception and use of color.'

'I would like to know more about how schools identify students as handicapped when students have no detectable physical or neurological impairments.'

Each of these statements reflects a beginning focus of inquiry that is exploratory and descriptive. In addition, each focus of inquiry provides the initial boundaries of the study, broadly indicating what types of information to include in data collection and what types of people or settings to seek for inclusion (or exclusion) in the study. We liken this to throwing out a wide net, so as to be more assured of gathering up the important aspects of the phenomenon under study about which we initially know little. Once the study is underway and initial data is analyzed, the net will narrow or perhaps expand or even be drawn to a new spot! Thus it is likely that your focus of inquiry will change — narrowing, expanding, or being redirected — as the salient aspects of the phenomenon under study become more clear. This is an important step in a qualitative research study: finding out what you need to find out more about (Lincoln and Guba, 1985).

Refer back to your concept map and the idea that most interested you. Develop a qualitative research question or statement using the sentence stem 'I would like to know more about . . .' or 'I would like to understand more about . . .' This is your initial focus of inquiry.

At this point in the development of a qualitative research study, a review of the relevant literature is in order, particularly if you are interested in working with an existing theory or body of work. Going to the research literature after developing a focus of inquiry may seem a bit out of sequence for individuals who have designed research studies using the traditional model of research, where one's hypothesis evolves out of studying the research related to one's topic. We have found, however, that for beginning qualitative researchers, a fresh approach to a topic of interest helps maintain an attitude of discovery and a broader focus of inquiry allowing for later narrowing or broadening of the focus as the data suggest it.

When searching the research literature on a topic, it is particularly useful if you can find relevant research that is qualitative, as evidenced by the eight features of qualitative research presented earlier. Quantitative studies can help inform you about your topic, but reliance on these studies presents the paradigm-fit problem: you are relying on research based on the postulates of a different paradigm. Developing a qualitative research study based on a theory or body of research that has resulted from a traditional approach to inquiry may yield quite incongruous findings.

Reference

LINCOLN, Y.S. and GUBA, E.G. (1985) *Naturalistic Inquiry*, Beverly Hills, CA: Sage.

Chapter 6

Building a Sample

Many of us have been taught that in order to have an acceptable sample for a research project, we should select people at random from the population. Randomness means that every person in the population of interest has an equal chance of being selected for inclusion in the study. A randomly selected sample serves an important purpose: it increases the likelihood that the sample accurately represents the population from which it was selected, allowing for results of the study to be generalized to the larger population. However, traditional quantitative researchers concerned with complex human phenomena rarely have the opportunity to select a truly random sample and often settle for approximations of randomness.

Qualitative researchers, on the other hand, set out to build a sample that includes people (or settings) selected with a different goal in mind: gaining deep understanding of some phenomenon experienced by a carefully selected group of people. This approach to purposefully selecting people (or settings, organizations) for a study acknowledges the complexity that characterizes human and social phenomena (Postulate I) and the limits of generalizabilty (Postulate III). There are several strategies for purposive sampling and the selection of a sampling strategy depends upon the focus of inquiry and the researcher's judgment as to which approach will yield the clearest understanding of the phenomena under study. Michael Quinn Patton (1990) suggests several sampling strategies that aim toward increased understanding versus generalizability of results. A researcher may choose to sample extreme cases (people or settings) to better understand some unusual phenomenon or because these cases may be particularly illuminating. On the other hand, a researcher may choose to select only typical cases when inquiry into atypical cases is beyond the boundaries of the study. Patton offers the strategy of sampling critical cases as a way to understanding the larger phenomena subsumed by the critical cases. But perhaps the most prominent and useful strategy is *maximum variation* sampling, where the researcher attempts to understand some phenomenon by seeking out persons or settings that represent the greatest differences in that phenomenon (Lincoln and Guba, 1985; Patton, 1990; Taylor and Bogdan, 1984).

Maximum variation sampling provides the qualitative researcher with a method by which the variability characteristic of random selection can be addressed, while recognizing that the goal of a qualitative study is not generalizability. It is not our goal to build a random sample, but rather to select persons or settings that we think represent the range of experience on the phenomenon in which we are interested. Thus, it is our working knowledge of the contexts of the individuals and settings that lead us to select them for initial inclusion in our study.

As we collect information from our first research participants and begin to analyze this data, we will learn what are the important or salient dimensions in the phenomenon we are studying. These preliminary results will suggest to us who or where to go next in our study by providing clues as to what is important to understand about the phenomenon. In building a sample, qualitative researchers may use a technique called *snowball* sampling, where one research participant or setting leads to another or snowballs. For the purpose of maximum variation, it is advisable for the qualitative researcher to use the snowball technique or other techniques to locate subsequent participants or settings that are very different from the first. In this way, maximum variation sampling is *emergent and sequential* (Lincoln and Guba, 1985). Glaser and Strauss (1976) call this sampling approach *theoretical sampling* because it allows the researcher to build and broaden theoretical insights in the ongoing process of data collection and analysis.

For example, suppose that we are interested in understanding more about students' experience of learning from lectures in college courses (our focus of inquiry). We want to purposefully select students to participate in our study who reflect the scope and range of students' experience of lectures as a method of college instruction. On what basis would we select students for our sample? How many students would we need to select to fully understand the phenomenon of learning from lectures? Where can we get help in answering these questions? First, we can see that our sample is broadly defined in the focus of inquiry: college students who are enrolled in one or more courses in which lecture is one of the methods of teaching. An operational definition of what constitutes a lecture would be an important next step, since the term lecture holds various meanings for teachers and students (Cerbin and Erickson, 1991). It would also be useful to check the research literature on this topic.

As it turns out, several qualitative studies of college students' experience of learning through lectures, essay-writing, reading, etc., have been conducted at Swedish and British Universities and polytechnics (Marton, Hounsell and Entwistle, 1984). The studies contained in the edited volume by Marton and associates, and other research we might find, would provide us with useful information on what has been discovered about students' learning from lectures, using the qualitative paradigm, and on qualitative methodology that might be appropriate for our own study. In Vivian Hodgson's (1984) study of learning from lectures, students at different stages of their college careers were selected from courses that were required for their degree and thus assumed to be relevant. In addition, students were selected based on the extent to which they thought the interpersonal qualities of the lecturer, such as, rapport with students, influenced their opinion of the relevance of the lectures more than impersonal perceptions, for example, 'very knowledgeable'.

To achieve maximum variation, Hodgson selected students who reported that they were most influenced by interpersonal factors, students who were least influenced by interpersonal factors, and students who reported being midway on this dimension. Her sample totaled 31 students and yielded useful information on the topic of student learning from lectures. By deliberately seeking to maximize the contrast among study participants on substantive characteristics, Hodgson and others have demonstrated the utility of purposive sampling.[1]

A second source of information that may help us decide whom to include in a study is 'experienced and knowledgeable experts' (Lincoln and Guba, 1985). In our study example above, who would be among the experienced and knowledgeable experts available to help us determine what types of students to initially include in our sample? We could, of course, ask several students what influences their experience of learning from lectures, and use these variables as part of our pool of ideas for sample selection. We could also ask teachers who lecture what differences among students they believe influence students' learning from their lectures. Combining these student and teacher perceptions with information from the research literature is likely to provide us with some very useful characteristics to use as a beginning guide for the purpose of maximum variation sampling.

Research exercise #6: Exploring the concept of maximum variation

Consider the focus of inquiry of the study example above: Understanding more about students' experience of learning from lectures in college courses. Engaging in the following exercise can help you identify what types of students you might want to include in your study (adapted from Lincoln and Guba, 1985).
    You will need pen and paper to carry our this exercise.

1 Imagine that you are a new student eager to do well in college. You have heard that many of the professors lecture as a main teaching strategy. You have been given a report describing other students' experiences of learning through lectures. The report contains a series of case studies, each case study describing in detail each student and what they thought and felt about lecture-learning. No attempt has been made in the report to generalize about how most students learn from lecture. On what basis would you decide which case study to read? What information would make the case study relevant for you? Write this information down on your paper.

2 For the second part of this exercise, you are to shift roles. Imagine you are a college professor who does some lecturing and is interested in improving his or her teaching. You receive a copy of the report from the academic dean. On what basis would you decide which case study to read? What information would make the case study relevant for you? Write this information down on your paper.

We have used this exercise with students in developing the criteria to use in building a purposive sample for several qualitative research studies. Taking the perspective of the potential consumers of the research report has yielded some useful sample selection characteristics that would otherwise have gone unidentified.

After we have exhausted our sources of information for building a sample relevant to our focus of inquiry, we can then take the variables we believe to be the most useful for initially building in variation and develop a sampling profile. In our study example, we might decide that the age of the student is particularly relevant to consider. The ability to connect new information with prior knowledge and experience is an important element in learning, and a student's age can be used to roughly approximate amount of experience. The increasing proportion of nontraditional students (aged 25 or over) entering or returning to college underscores the relevance of age as an important starting point.

A second variable that is likely to be important in understanding students' experience of learning from lectures is specific content knowledge. Here again we are considering the importance of prior knowledge for understanding new information. Involving students in our study who are at different points in their degree programs (i.e., year in school) would be one way to build in variations in specific prior knowledge. We would want to try to understand the students' experience of learning from lectures in the content areas for which they have more or less prior knowledge.

A third variable that is likely to come up in a study on learning is gender. A growing body of qualitative research suggests that there are gender differences in how knowledge is received, understood, and integrated (Belenky, Clinchy, Goldberger and Tarule, 1986; Marton *et al.*, 1984; Perry, 1970). Thus, to fully understand the phenomenon of learning from lecture, we would probably want to involve both women and men in our study. Taken together, the variables of age, year in school, and gender can be used to build initial profiles of students we would want to seek out for initial inclusion in our study. For example, we would want to involve a male student, age 18 or 19, who is in his first year of a mathematics degree, a female student, between 25 and 35 years of age who is in her final year of a business degree, and so on. Note, however, that we are not trying to select a student who satisfies every permutation of our three variables. Rather, we are using the three variables as a guide for selection, as we begin our study.

Thinking out loud about the sample for a qualitative research study and building the sample in this manner can raise important questions about one's focus of inquiry. Is it too broad? Should we bind the study more tightly in order to make it more manageable? Is it too narrow? Should we open it up to allow for more unknowns to emerge? In our study example we might wonder whether we want to investigate learning from lectures in all courses of study or limit our inquiry to a more specific field of study, such as engineering, biology, or philosophy. We might also wonder whether we should limit our study to one gender or the other, or to one age group or another. These considerations, like other aspects of qualitative research, challenge the qualitative researcher to refine the focus of inquiry based on his or her own interests, research capabilities and resources, and the existing qualitative research literature.

Research exercise #7: Developing a beginning guide for sample selection

The purpose of this exercise is to identify variables that you could use in building a sample for your own study, using maximum variation sampling.
    You will need paper and pen to carry out this exercise.

1   Return to the focus of inquiry you developed in *Research exercise #6*. Write this at the top of your paper.
2   What broadly-defined sample is indicated by your focus of inquiry? Write this sample description under your focus of inquiry. Your sample may be made up of a defined group of people, such as teenagers, parents, employees, managers, etc., or defined settings, such as schools, social service agencies, businesses, specific programs.
3   Among the sample participants or settings, what important differences exist that are important for you to consider for the focus of your inquiry? Try several techniques to answer this question:

   a) Return to *Research exercise #5*. Who are the potential consumers of the report that results from your study? Who would really be interested in the outcomes of your inquiry? On what basis would these consumers decide whether or not to read your study? On what basis would these consumers decide which part (or case study) to read in your report? Keep a record of your ideas.
   b) Who are the experienced and knowledgeable experts on your topic? Researchers and theorists who publish work on your topic are certainly among

the knowledgeable experts. A library search may yield useful information on your topic, particularly if you can locate relevant studies that were conducted using the alternate paradigm and qualitative methodology. What do the studies suggest about your focus that might help you in deciding whom to include in your sample?

c) Who are the experienced and knowledgeable experts on your topic who are close to home? Faculty members of colleges and universities, practitioners in applied fields and informed members of the community may be sources of useful information and ideas on your topic. You might ask these individuals who or what they would study in order to understand more about your topic. You might ask them to participate in an exercise, such as the one you completed for *Research exercise #5*, in order to expand their thinking on the topic. Remember, however, that most people, including college faculty, have had relatively little formal training in qualitative research and are likely to approach your study from a conventional research perspective.

d) What do you know about the phenomenon you are trying to understand more about? Do not overlook your own working knowledge of what you are interested in studying. Record your own ideas on who or what to study that will provide you with the broadest range of information possible.

4 Look carefully over your notes from step 3. Identify three to five key variables that you think will provide the maximum contrast among sample participants (or settings) and yield the widest range of information on the topic you are studying. Then, develop a series of profiles of the potential persons or settings that you would like to be able to investigate. *The profiles serve as guides for sample selection.* A profile is created by checking various combinations of the key variables. The profile shown in Figure 6.1 is based on our study example, using in-depth interviews as the method of data collection.

The use of profiles for sample selection provides a starting place for a qualitative study. But in contrast to conventional models of research design, we cannot specify who will comprise our final sample, since we have not yet discovered what is most important to know about the phenomenon we are studying, or who are the best people to inform our understanding. We have made a best guess about where to start in our development of the profiles. But it is the joint and ongoing process of sample selection and data analysis that will guide our emergent research design (Lincoln and Guba, 1985). As our focus of inquiry guides us in our initial sample selection, the early and ongoing analysis of the data will suggest what is important to explore further. We would then seek participants (or settings) that can further illuminate our new understanding.

Sample Size

You may have noticed that the size of Hodgson's (1984) sample of college students was relatively small — 31 students — based on traditional scientific standards. The question of sample size is a critical component of conventional studies because it directly influences the

Figure 6.1: A possible profile for the study example: Understanding more about students' experience of learning from lectures

LEARNING FROM LECTURES RESEARCH PROJECT
Purposive Sampling Profile

Please locate an interviewee who matches as closely as possible the profile indicated below. By interviewing individuals who represent different profiles, we will get closer to achieving maximum variation. The profiles are based on the variables we identified as important for our focus of inquiry.

Age
☐ 18–19 years
☐ 20–21 years
☐ 22–25 years
☐ 26–30 years
☐ over 30 years

Year in School
☐ first (freshman)
☐ second (sophomore)
☐ third (junior)
☐ fourth (senior)

Gender
☐ female
☐ male

*Degree Program**
☐ Natural Sciences or Health Sciences
☐ Social Sciences or Education
☐ Humanities
☐ Business
☐ Computer Sciences

* All degree programs include required
courses which are taught primarily
through lecture.

robustness of the statistical tests used to measure the significance of numerical data and the generalizability of study results. There are numerous formulas that can be used to estimate what size sample is needed in order to detect a significant finding, if in fact one exists.

On what basis does the qualitative researcher determine sample size? We cannot decide a priori how many people or settings we must include in our study in order to fully understand the phenomenon of interest. Ideally, we continue to jointly collect data and analyze it in an ongoing process until we uncover no new information. We continue to gather information until we reach the saturation point, when newly collected data is redundant with previously collected data. (Glaser and Strauss, 1967; Guba, 1978). In other words, when we reach a point of diminishing returns from our data collection efforts, we can be reasonably assured that we have conducted a thorough study. Lincoln and Guba

(1985) state that a carefully conducted study, where sample selection has been emergent and sequential, can reach the saturation point with as few as twelve participants and probably no more than twenty. From his own research, Douglas (1985) estimated that in-depth interviews with twenty-five people were necessary before he reached the saturation point. Practically speaking, the sampling concepts of saturation of information and diminishing returns may have to be balanced with limitations of time, money, and other factors that impinge upon the research enterprise.

Preparing a Qualitative Research Proposal: Getting Started

With an understanding of the qualitative approach to doing research and strategies for developing a focus of inquiry and a beginning sample, you can begin to design a research study of your own. In the subsequent chapters you will learn about qualitative methods of data collection, and how to analyze qualitative data which will allow you to add to your design.

Unlike the traditional approaches to research design, the components of qualitative research proposal have not been precisely articulated by researchers, or by colleges or funding agencies who approve research projects. We offer two examples of qualitative research proposals in the Appendix. The first example was submitted by us to a local school district and was prepared according to the format required by the district. This proposal was accepted and the research was carried out to the satisfaction of the school district. The second proposal example was developed by two students who were interested in exploring the lives of children with autism who are using a new communication technique known as 'facilitated communication'. Their proposal illustrates the main components we suggest in a qualitative research proposal, which are discussed below.

Problem Statement

In a clear and direct way state your focus of inquiry and provide a rationale for pursuing this topic. It is important to demonstrate some of your scholarship here by briefly reviewing a sample of the relevant literature, including a brief description of the research approaches used. You may find yourself pursuing a topic for which no qualitative studies have been done and this will be important to point out. Or perhaps you may propose a research project that you hope will contribute to a growing body of qualitative research on the topic of interest. It is your task to provide a convincing rationale for why your study needs to be done.

Focus of Inquiry

Provide a clear statement of your focus of inquiry, presented in the form of a research(s) question or statement.

Research Design

The design of a research study includes the overall approach to be taken and detailed information about how the study will be carried out, with whom and where. A concise statement about the overarching research design is often missing or hard to discern in published reports of qualitative research. We suggest that you inform the reader that you are proposing a *qualitative* research study, and provide some explanation about what this means. (The eight characteristics of qualitative research outlined in Chapter 4 will be helpful here.) Specifically, you will want to make clear whether your research design is *emergent* or *nonemergent*. An emergent research design means that you will begin with an initial focus of inquiry and an initial sample, and refine your focus of inquiry and sampling strategy as you engage in an ongoing process of data collection and analysis (Lincoln and Guba, 1985). A nonemergent research design means you will pursue your focus of inquiry with qualitative methods of data collection and data analysis, but that you will collect data, *then* analyze it. A nonemergent design is less desirable than one that is emergent, but it can yield important information and suggest a direction for subsequent data collection efforts.

Within your discussion of the research design, it is important to include *provisions for trustworthiness*. Trustworthiness is the term used by Lincoln and Guba (1985) to refer to the believability of a researcher's findings. What has the researcher done in designing, carrying out, and reporting his or her study that persuades us that the results are credible? The methodology presented in this book includes many steps that will increase the trustworthiness of a qualitative research study. In Chapter 10 we will specifically discuss this topic.

Methods

There are several components that should be included in the methods section of a qualitative research proposal: sampling strategy and the people or settings that will make up the sample, data collection procedures and procedures for data analysis. In an emergent research design, the researcher will not be able to specify exactly what will happen, but it is possible to present procedural information about the proposed study.

Sample

In this chapter you read about building a purposive sample using a strategy known as maximum variation sampling. Patton (1990) discusses other approaches you might want to use. In this section you want to describe your sampling strategy and, if you are using an emergent research design, describe which types of persons or settings you will initially seek out for your sample. You may already have obtained permission to interview a few people who meet your criteria, or have obtained access to a setting you want to observe. This would be important information to include in your discussion of the sample.

You will not be able to specify the size of your sample if you are using an emergent design, but you can describe for the reader your basis for terminating sampling, for example, reaching the saturation point. There are, however, a few exceptions. If you are only proposing to study the experiences of one person, as in life history research, or you will explore one setting in depth, then obviously you will have a sample size of one. A second exception is when you have assessed your personal resources of time, money and other factors, and decide you cannot include more than a relatively fixed number of people or settings. This was the case for the student researchers whose proposal appears in the Appendix. They were quite certain that an in-depth study of four children was all they could accomplish over a six month period. As you will note, however, in their proposal they included a request to increase the size of the sample in a possible continuation of the study.

Data collection methods

In the next chapter you will read about the major methods of data collection used in qualitative research: participant observation, in-depth interviewing, and document analysis. In this section of the proposal you want to describe the methods you plan to use and a rationale for your choice. We also suggest that since the researcher is the human instrument collecting and analyzing qualitative data, it is appropriate to report information about this person(s), particularly as it relates to the focus of inquiry. At minimum, we believe researchers should report their gender, education and training and any personal experience that is especially relevant to the study. For example, if you were exploring people's experience with a business's employee assistance program and you had been an employee of that same business, this information would be important to report.

Data Analysis Procedures

There are several ways to approach the analysis of qualitative data that vary in the level of interpretation engaged in by the researcher. There are also several specific techniques that can be used to search for meaning in the data. In Chapter 10 we will discuss one approach to the data — to accurately describe what has been studied — and one technique for analyzing qualitative data known as the 'constant comparative method'. Whichever data analytic technique you plan to use in your study, explain it to the reader.

Reporting the Outcomes

In the last section of the proposal, discuss how you will inform others of your work. This is often in the form of a written report, but reporting can also be done through a presentation to the research participants or other appropriate audiences.

References

Submit a complete list of the references cited in the proposal.

Appendix

You may have materials that are most appropriately placed in an Appendix, such as an interview schedule. A copy of the researcher's resume might also be included. Note that each item that appears in the Appendix should also be referred to in the proposal.

Note

1 Hodgson's (1984) study revealed that university students experience the importance of lecture content in primarily three ways: intrinsically (important for deep and personal reasons), extrinsically (important for evaluation purposes) or vicariously (important because the lecturer maintains students' interest).

References

BELENKY, M.F., CLINCHY, B.M., GOLDBERGER, N.R. and TARULE, J.M. (1986) *Women's Ways of Knowing: The Development of Self, Voice and Mind*, New York: Basic Books.

CERBIN, W. and ERICKSON, C. (1991) University professors' perspectives on teaching, Unpublished data.

DOUGLAS, J. (1985) *Creative Interviewing*, Beverly Hills, CA: Sage.

GLASER, B.G. and STRAUSS, A.L. (1967) *The Discovery of Grounded Theory*, Chicago, IL: Aldine.

GUBA, E. (1978) *Toward a Methodology of Naturalistic Inquiry in Educational Evaluation*, Monograph 8, Los Angeles, CA: UCLA Center for the Study of Evaluation.

HODGSON, V. (1984) 'Learning from lectures', in MARTON, F., HOUNSELL, D. and ENTWISTLE, N. (Eds) *The Experience of Learning*, Edinburgh: Scottish Academic Press, pp. 90–102.

LINCOLN, Y.S. and GUBA, E.G. (1985) *Naturalistic Inquiry*, Beverly Hills, CA: Sage.

MARTON, F., HOUNSELL, D. and ENTWISTLE, N. (Eds) (1984) *The Experience of Learning*, Edinburgh: Scottish Academic Press.

PATTON, M.Q. (1990) *Qualitative Evaluation and Research Methods* (2nd ed.), Newbury Park, CA: Sage.

PERRY, W.G. (1970) *Forms of Intellectual and Ethical Development in the College Years: A Scheme*, New York: Holt, Rinehart, and Winston.

TAYLOR, S.T. and BOGDAN, R. (1984) *Introduction to Qualitative Research Methods: The Search for Meanings* (2nd ed.), New York: Wiley.

Chapter 7

Data Collection in the Natural Setting: Studying People, Studying Settings

---

In a famous quotation, Urie Bronfenbrenner, the noted child psychologist, stated that the overemphasis on laboratory studies in developmental psychology has unfortunately led to 'the science of strange behavior of children in strange situations with strange adults for the briefest possible periods of time' (1979: 19). In this statement Bronfenbrenner points to the importance of the alternate paradigm and qualitative research methodology in coming to an understanding of human experience. In order to understand any human phenomenon we must investigate it as part of the context within which it lies (see Table 2.1). The postulates that define the alternate paradigm lead quite directly to the methods available to the qualitative researcher to use in real or natural settings. In this and succeeding chapters we will direct our attention to three major qualitative data collection methods: participant observation, in-depth interviews, and group interviews. We will also briefly discuss documents and other sources of qualitative data. Each method attempts to capture people's words and actions, the data of qualitative research. But whatever methods of data collection are chosen, the researcher will benefit by maintaining a researcher's journal.

The Researcher's Journal

In several books about qualitative research methods, experienced researchers discuss their practice of writing notes to themselves as an integral part of the research process (Glaser and Strauss, 1967; Lincoln and Guba, 1985, Taylor and Bogdan, 1984). These notes are variously referred to as a diary, a journal, or as memos, and contain the researcher's personal record of insights, beginning understandings, working hunches, recurring words or phrases, ideas, questions, thoughts, concerns and decisions made during the research process. We encourage beginning researchers to maintain a research journal from the beginning to the end of their research project. A richly detailed research journal becomes a useful part of the data collection and analysis process.

Participant Observation

Historically it has been the cultural anthropologist who has developed and refined the method of qualitative data collection called *participant observation*. Famous cultural anthropologists such as Margaret Mead and Ruth Benedict have sought to understand the lives of people *in their own terms* by spending extended amounts of time with people in the natural settings they inhabit. Anthropologists' efforts at describing culture or aspects of culture is called ethnography, and there are numerous ethnographic accounts of the lives of people in diverse settings, climates, and stages of development (Boas, 1911; Malinowski, 1932; Mead, 1960). Participant observation also has a rich tradition in sociology and education. More recently Robert Coles (1989) John Holt (1964, 1967), and Jonathon Kozol (1986) have provided illuminating accounts of students' school experiences and pointed the way to important educational reforms. It is from these early ethnographers that we have learned about being a participant observer.

The participant observer attempts to enter the lives of others, to indwell, in Polanyi's term, suspending as much as possible his or her own ways of viewing the world. In the broadest sense, the participant observer asks the questions: What is happening here? What is important in the lives of people here? How would they describe their lives and what is the language they would use to do it? The task is one of listening hard and keenly observing what is going on among people in a given situation or organization or culture in an effort to more deeply understand it and them. Relying again on emergent research design, the participant observer begins with a broad focus of inquiry and through the ongoing process of observing and participating in the setting, recording what she sees and hears, and analyzing the data, salient aspects of the setting emerge. Subsequent observations are guided by initial discoveries.

Using participant observation for qualitative research is for many the method of choice (Patton, 1990). It is also the method of data collection which draws most heavily upon the various skills of the qualitative researcher. As Norman Denzin (1978) notes, participant observation 'simultaneously combines document analysis, interviewing of respondents and informants, direct participation and observation, and introspection' (p. 183). In addition, gaining access to the setting we want to begin studying often requires tact and persistence. Being in and of the setting while also observing it, stretches our interpersonal and information-processing skills. And the prolonged engagement, over weeks or months, necessary to understand others-in-context taxes the energies of even the most experienced researchers. It is possible, however, to draw on many of the skills you probably already possess to develop your skills as a participant observer.

Gaining Access

In anthropology, psychology, and other fields debate continues about the use of *overt* as compared to *covert* means of gaining access to research participants and settings. We, along with other qualitative researchers, have adopted the view that deceptive and covert practices are not in keeping with ethical practice or postulates of the alternative paradigm (Taylor and Bogdan, 1984; Lincoln and Guba, 1985; Shils, 1959). We view the participants in the research study as essentially collaborators who together with us mutually shape and determine what we come to understand about them and their situation (Postulate II).

A study conducted by Edwin Farrell and his associates exemplifies the participant-as-collaborator approach to research (Farrell, Peguero, Lindsey and White, 1988). Farrell was involved in the development of a drop-out prevention program, jointly begun by The City College of New York and several high schools in the city of New York. But prior to setting up the prevention program, the research group focused on the need to more deeply understand the students at risk for dropping out. In their words,

> To set up a viable program, it was necessary to gain some understanding of the population we were dealing with that went beyond attendance records, test scores, promotion records, and guidance referrals. First, we needed to know what the lives of the students were like and how school fitted into those lives.
> (Farrell *et al.*, 1988: 489)

Finding the traditional quantitative approaches ill-matched and inappropriate to conducting an 'inquiry into the lives of the students' (p. 490), Farrell turned to qualitative research methods, initially interested in becoming a participant observer in school. But his ability to 'become invisible' was compromised, in his view, by being 'a white, middle-class, middle-aged academic entering a social setting made up, for the most part, of low-income black and Hispanic adolescents' (p. 490). Farrell also believed his sociocultural differences from the sample would limit his ability to fully analyze the data.

The solution Farrell arrived at illuminates the possibilities of collaborative qualitative research. From a pool of several students who met the criteria for being at risk for dropping out of high school, seven students were recruited as collaborators in the research effort, and three of these students were involved for the duration of the study (see the last three names in the reference citation). Farrell's high school collaborators tape recorded informal interviews with other students and analyzed interview transcripts in conjunction with Farrell. The outcomes of the study revealed the depth of students' overwhelming experience of competing social pressures and the experience of school as yet another source of pressure. Boredom was also an important theme, and interpreted by the first author to be perhaps 'a way of internally dropping out of school' (Farrell *et al.*, 1988).

In his writings, Elliot Mishler (1986), a social psychologist and qualitative researcher emphasizes the importance of reducing the power differential between the researcher and the research participants by involving the participants as collaborators. The study by Farrell and his research team exemplifies the possibilities for collaboration. However, researchers who view participants as partners rather than subjects in the research process may be seen by traditional researchers as running the risk of revealing the purpose of the study, thus influencing the validity of the results. This concern reflects a basic difference between the traditional and alternative paradigms that guide our modes of inquiry. Proponents of the alternative qualitative paradigm assume that rapport established with study participants through open and honest exchange is essential to indwelling and to achieving useful study outcomes. While many other books on qualitative research present the overt-to-covert continuum and leave it to the researcher to decide, we clearly choose to err on the side of disclosure.

Adoption of an overt approach to gaining access mean that the researcher approaches the key individuals or gatekeepers (Becker, 1970) of the setting willing to share her or his focus of inquiry. As the study proceeds the researcher may involve study participants by asking for assistance in locating certain other individuals or settings that are emerging as important aspects of the phenomenon under study. Participants might also be asked to respond to preliminary patterns and themes that have developed out of the data analysis. Finally, the research participants are invited to review the outcomes of the study to determine whether the researcher has captured the reality of their experiences.

Several researchers 'negotiate the outcomes' of their study with the research participants, and will not report outcomes that have not been agreed to by the participants (Lincoln and Guba, 1985). This ongoing involvement with study participants highlights the importance of overt approaches to gaining access from the very beginning of the study.

Being There

Participant observation, by definition, requires the researcher to be in the field or present in the natural settings where the phenomenon under study takes place. We can get a glimpse of a kind of participant observer from a popular film in the 1970s entitled *Being There*. The actor Peter Sellars poignantly portrays Chance Gardener, a man who is mentally retarded. In essence, Chance takes literally what other characters say and responds with an endearing *naïveté* to their statements and requests, a *naïveté* which endears him to the other characters. Chance also is a keen observer, who speaks rarely but deliberately. We might think of Chance as a kind of participant observer who is by all accounts 'being there', functioning without interpretation, taking in through sight and sound what is unfolding.

The challenge to the qualitative researcher of being there is complicated by the task of also becoming invisible, as a researcher (Berg, 1989; Stoddart, 1986). The qualitative researcher assumes that his or her presence will be reacted to by the participants in the setting to some extent, but by assuming an unobtrusive presence the researcher minimizes this reactivity. Primarily through the process of prolonged engagement that the participant observer's researcher status becomes less prominent, as evidenced in the participants' conversation and behavior. Stoddart (1986) notes that becoming invisible is facilitated by participating in the ongoing activities of the participants, without calling particular attention to oneself, rather than adopting the posture of a detached researcher seeking objectivity.

But how much should one participate or try to fit into the setting and with the participants one is studying? This is not a simple decision, nor one that necessarily remains constant throughout the study. Once again we are guided by Polanyi's concept of indwelling. What will dictate how much we are a participant and how much we are an observer at any given moment is our judgment of what it takes to understand the situation from the inside out. In Patton's words, 'The challenge is to combine participation and observation so as to become capable of understanding the program [setting, participants] as an insider while describing the program for outsiders' (1990: 128). This is often a delicate balance, one that becomes easier to achieve with experience.

Field Notes

The keen observations and important conversations one has in the field cannot be fully utilized in a rigorous analysis of the data unless they are written down. *The qualitative researcher's field notes contain what has been seen and heard by the researcher, without interpretation.* In other words, the participant observer's primary task is to record what happened without inferring feelings to the participants (e.g., 'Patty looked bored'.) and without inferring why or how something happened (e.g., 'I think Jeff is trying to impress Patty'.). These hunches are important to take note of, but the researcher's interpretation of events must be clearly set off from observations. This can be done quite easily by using brackets or parentheses to indicate commentary by the participant observer. Some researchers also use the initials *OC* to indicate observer's comments in their field notes (Taylor and Bogdan, 1984). The student researcher who provided the field notes example shown in Figure 7.1 used brackets to distinguish her commentary from what she observed in the field.

How does one go about being invisible and take copious notes about what one is experiencing? In many situations it means being exceptionally alert in the field, knowing that you will need to write down what you have seen and heard in great detail after you leave the setting. Sometimes it is possible to unobtrusively excuse yourself from the setting and privately jot down some of the observations you want to be able to recall later. Additionally, it has been our experience that people are usually quite willing to have informal interviews with participant observers, when it is clearly communicated that what they have to say is important and that writing their words down will help the researcher remember. This possibility is likely to be enhanced when people perceive themselves as collaborators in the research effort.

Preparing useful field notes is a challenging task, one which is facilitated by taking considerable time to write immediately after one leaves the field. Many researchers begin their field notes by jotting down bits of information they want to recall, such as interesting terms and ideas they have heard or read, behaviors that were particularly unusual, and noteworthy objects in the environment. These bits of information can then be organized into a kind of narrative of what was observed, usually approximating a chronological ordering.

It is often useful to draw a diagram of the physical layout of the

Figure 7.1: Excerpt from the field notes of a student researcher who was able to take notes during the observation

The setting is a large lecture class taking place at a local university. Note that the researcher uses brackets to her own commentary from her actual observations.

[12:42pm] The teacher then switched to what the class would be doing that day, she said something like 'lots of book talk today'. Two young women in the front row started talking to one another while the teacher was talking. Several people [maybe 5] were shifting around in their desks. The teacher then was talking about '. . . catching up with response logs today'.

One young man in the row in front of me was paging through the *Wings For the Future* brochure. Another female student, two rows in front of me was paging through another kind of book. Three students in that same row on the far right were paging through notebooks. The teacher said something like: 'You are doing a wonderful job with your personal responses.' [She had described them as journals for personal reactions to the material they were covering in class and the text.] The teacher went on to say I think '. . . journals now will be taken on a rotation basis . . .' [I find myself concentrating on what the teacher is saying rather than on the class participants].

[12:46pm] Two young women sitting in front of me were discussing something. I haven't seen any of the students write anything down yet. Most people have notebooks or binders sitting on their desks. Some are open and some are closed. Three to four different groups of student pairs are talking to one another while the teacher is talking. The teacher now is talking about '. . . have to remember that you have a life outside of school. It's easy to be a martyr . . . if something comes up outside of school you have to take care of yourself . . . I've seen a lot of teacher burn-out from not taking care of yourself.' [The teacher I think is referring to once the students are teachers, not their role presently as students.]

[12:49pm] Now about half of the class is looking up at the teacher and the other half of the class is looking down at either their notebooks or binders open on their desk. A young man — two desks down from me in the same row — eyes are closed [he appears to be sleeping]. The teacher is saying something like, 'Nancy Atwall, a teacher in New Hampshire . . . an 8th grade middle school teacher . . . holistic teaching'. A young woman in front of me is looking at the *Focus* brochure. The young woman sitting next to her is looking down and is picking at her fingernails. The young man whose eyes were closed reaches down and gets his notebook out of a bag on the floor.

[12:52pm] The fourth woman in from the aisle in the row directly in front of me is paging through the *Wings For the Future* brochure. The teacher continues to give a personal history of Nancy Atwall. [I'm finding it difficult to listen to the teacher and observe the class at the same time — should I focus on one or another?] The teacher says something like, '. . . I want to make teaching fun and I don't ever want to stop doing that.'

[12:56pm] [I stopped to figure out how many rows and desks were filled in the classroom. I thought it might help me remember more when I typed up the fieldnotes if I could reference where people were sitting.] A young woman who the teacher called Jean asked a question, 'Are you saying then we will get stuff back from our personal journals?' The teacher said something like, '. . . yes and I will share also, many times presentations start out in your journal.' [I don't know what this all had to do with the Nancy Atwall stuff — now I wish I had been listening to the teacher instead of counting rows and desks!]. The teacher is now talking about publishing and says something like '. . . publishing is sharing publicly in some way . . . that's all it is.'

Figure 7.2: Map from a middle school cafeteria completed as part of the student researcher's field notes

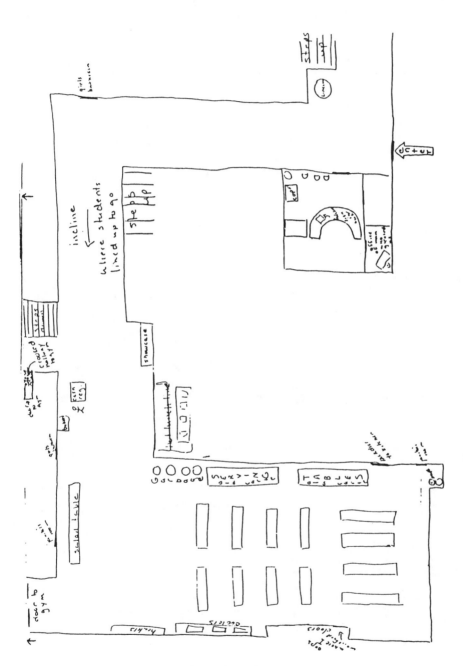

Note: Examples of student work appear throughout the book. This work is at times not completely legible, but we think these examples serve an important illustrative purpose.

setting in as much detail as possible, noting such things as where people stood or sat, important objects, unused spaces, traffic patterns, etc. This type of diagram can also aid one's recall of events and conversations at the time of preparing field notes and possibly later on. Note also that the map itself, as part of the field notes, is data and will be used in data analysis. One such map from the study of adolescents' experiences in a middle school cafeteria is shown in Figure 7.2.

As much as possible, the researcher tries to capture people's exact words in the field notes. This is particularly important because the qualitative researcher is specifically trying to understand and describe what is going on in the terms used by the people in the setting she or he is studying. In addition, the researcher cannot assume that the terms used by the people in the setting mean the same to them as they do to the researcher. In the study described above, Farrell and his young collaborators (1988) discovered that *boredom* was a term used to describe classes that had a boring routine, that the *process* of handing back assignments, giving assignments, quizzes, etc. defined whether a class was boring. In discussing this finding, Farrell noted that he related boredom to the *content* of academic classes. Uncovering the students' meaning of boredom was pivotal in this study.

The researcher attempts to provide the clearest and most complete narrative of what went on in the field. People's actions and interactions are described. Outside intrusions, such as an alarm going off or phone call are noted. Verbatim words or statements are recorded using quotation marks. Statements that are a reconstruction or paraphrasing of a person's words are written down without using quotation marks. Observer's comments are added in a way that sets them off from the descriptive narrative. An example of field notes prepared after being in the field are shown in Figure 7.3.

Figure 7.3: Excerpt from the field notes of a student researcher who recorded her notes after an observation in the middle school cafeteria

Field Notes for Lincoln Middle School Feb. 12, 1992

I walked toward the school looking for the door to go into. Everything outside was quiet. I grasped the handle of the nearest door that I came to, but it was locked. Through the glass of this door, I could see the area that the students would be eating in, set up with tables, chairs, and food being put out in the serving areas.

I proceeded to the 9th Street door, and entered the school. The hall that I walked into was very noisy from the students that filled its halls as they were going to or were by their lockers. I looked to the left and saw a sign on a door that said main office, so I entered this room. Here there were about three grown-ups behind desks or in offices and one child sitting in a chair just inside the door. One woman was using the photocopier machine and was talking to the child who then took the completed copies and left the room.

I looked for someone to ask for guidance, but there was no one behind the main desk. To the left there was a large office with a rather large-framed man walking toward me. He was talking, but not to me. I then saw my classmate, Mike Premo, and understood that the man was talking to Mike, who had arrived just before I did. [*OC:* I assume that the man in the office is probably a principal or vice-principal, although I was not introduced.] Mike pointed to the folder that we signed up in, and I proceeded to check-in.

When I was finished with this procedure, I joined in the conversation that Mike was having with the man. The man was asking about exactly what we would be doing, although he also said that he had read the information sent to the school regarding the project. He then informed us that we were more than welcome to purchase a hot lunch or ala carte meal from the cafeteria. Finally, he explained to us that one of the classes was on a skiing trip, so today we would be able to interact with only two classes, the 7th and 8th grades. We thanked him for his help and were on our way.

We left the office and turned left, following a group of students down the hall. As we neared the end of the hall, we could hear the loudness of the children talking. We entered the lunchroom, took a few seconds to scan the room, and separated, each taking seats at different areas of the room. I went up to a girl at a table and asked if she minded if I sat with her. She very quietly said 'no', so I sat next to her. There were two girls at my end of the table, and there were about six at the other end.

The two girls said nothing to me at this point, so I looked around the room. I noticed that the tables were set in an order, and that once a student had his/her food, they did not seem to scan the room for a friend, but went directly to a table [*OC* as if predetermined or assigned]. There were tables to my right that had ala carte type food such as chips, rolls, and juice.

Sometimes it is possible to take notes in the field as things are happening. In some situations, taking notes is the normal thing to be doing. For example, being a participant observer in a college classroom where the professor is lecturing — and students are implicitly or explicitly directed to take notes — it is possible to develop an ongoing record of what is happening. The field notes from one such experience are provided in Figure 7.1. Notice that in the field notes example it was possible for the participant observer to note the time when things actually occurred, allowing for estimates of the duration of activities to be drawn from the field notes. Of course, not all classrooms lend themselves to on-the-spot recording of sights and sounds. A classroom session devoted primarily to discussion is likely to make the fervent recordings of the researcher quite visible.

Research exercise #8: Observing without interpreting

The purpose of Research exericses #8 and #9 is to help you begin to hone your skills as a participant observer. The skill emphasized in this exercise is observing without interpreting.

You will need a substantial amount of paper, and pens that allow you to write easily to carry out this exercise.

1 Arrange to sit in on a class at a local college, university, or technical school. If you are currently in one of these places, try to conduct your participant observation in a course in which you are not currently enrolled. It is also helpful for this exercise to observe in a class where students are likely to be taking notes, and where your note-taking would not be unusual. Gaining access to classes is often

quite easy. You may be able to go with a friend or simply ask the instructor if you can sit in on a class 'to understand what it is like to be in this class' (focus of inquiry).

2   Go to the class equipped with paper and pens. If students can sit anywhere, try to sit in a place that is in the middle of things, rather than on the far outside edge or in the back of the room. Seating yourself outside the place where most students sit emphasizes your outsider status. On the other hand you may find that you have taken someone's seat, as it often happens that without any formal designation, students label a chair as theirs. In any case, notice what happens.

3   As you sit in the class, you will probably be more of an observer than a participant. Focus on what is going on and not on what you think about what is going on. Write down behavioural descriptions: No one raises their hand in response to the instructor asking, 'Anybody have any ideas about Sternberg's theory of intelligence?' Make a diagram of the classroom, including where students sit, where the instructor sits or stands, where the clock is, etc. Note the time you are taking notes and keep a running log of the time on your field notes (see Figure 7.1). Record what happens in the class in as much detail as possible. Use your diagram to locate students who talk or otherwise come to your attention. Chart the movement of the teacher throughout the class period. Capture in as much detail as possible what is going on. While it is not necessary to take precise notes about the course content, it would be helpful to note the progression of topics being presented and discussed.

4   You are likely to get ideas and wonder about what is happening in the setting, and your field notes can accommodate your thinking. For example, you may find yourself wondering why the instructor stands on the left side of the classroom while almost everyone else sits on the right. Or you may notice that a few people have their heads down, pen poised, but are actually asleep, and wonder whether the early hour of the class is an important factor in understanding what goes on. These types of observer comments can and should be entered into your field notes as you think of them by using parentheses, brackets, or O.C.: obsever's comment (see Figure 7.1).

5   After completing the field observation, take some time to review your notes. Add any observations you have omitted. Study your notes. Then on a separate page respond to the following questions: What is important here? What is it that I need to find out more about? What would I want to focus on more closely if I returned to this setting?

6   Finally, evaluate your experience of being a participant observer and preparing on-the-spot fieldnotes. Were you able to separate description from interpretation? Could someone reading your notes (typed) gain some understanding of what was happening in the class? Positive responses to these questions reflect the skilled use of participant observation.

One female student who completed this exercise had an unusual and funny experience. While she was sitting in a large lecture hall, another student unknown to her, turned to her, addressing her correctly as 'Sue'. The student then proceeded to ask the research student researcher about the last lecture, which she had missed, and whether she could borrow her notes. This exchange went on for awhile (as the lecturer talked on), until the research student corrected the case of mistaken identity. The advice this student gave to the rest of us will serve any participant observer well: Be prepared for the unexpected!

Research exercise #9: Reconstructing observations from the field

Rather than being able to take notes as one observes, the participant observer is more often required to recall the setting, participants, events, and conversations in detail after leaving the field. The purpose of this exercise is to practice this important skill.

1   Think about some settings or places you would like to know more about by being in that setting. A medical clinic? Backstage at a theater? A day care center? A senior citizen's community center? Make a list of these places.

2   Examine your list and identify a setting to which you have some reasonable chance of gaining access. Prepare a focus of inquiry statement that you can communicate to the gatekeepers of the setting. For example, 'I would like to know more about what it's like backstage while a performance is going on.' Or, 'I would like to understand what a senior center is like.'

3   Try to make the necessary arrangements to visit the setting for one hour. In some situations you will only need to ask; people will be delighted — flattered — at your interest in them. In other cases, it may be more difficult to gain entry into the setting. If you are unable to access the setting you are interested in through honest disclosure of your focus of inquiry, do not resort to covert or deceptive practices. Return to your list and find a setting that you can observe.

4   Spend one hour in the setting as a participant observer. Take a small note pad with you but do not take notes in the setting in which you are observing. If possible you can briefly excuse yourself from the setting and find a bathroom or other private location to jot down a few of your observations. Be alert and aware of what is going on there, trying to take in the whole situation, rather than arbitrarily picking some smaller corner, person or group to observe. Be aware of when you feel you need to be an observer and when you feel you need to participate, in order to gain an insider's view of this setting.

5   Immediately after leaving the setting and preferably before driving home or talking to anyone, reconstruct your observations. Begin by jotting down bits of what you heard and saw. Write down as closely as possible what people said. Record exact words and statements that you remember. Draw a detailed diagram of the setting. Then go back through your notes and develop a descriptive account of what happened in the setting while you were there, including such things as a description of the people you saw and heard, where you were, what happened and when, etc. Add observer's comments [*OC*]: your own musings, questions, and hunches about the place. Write clearly enough so that if you were lucky you could have someone else type up your field notes.

6   Carefully reread your field notes, guided by these questions: What is important here? What is it that I need to find out more about? What would I want to focus on more closely if I returned to this setting? Your responses to these questions would allow you to refine your focus on your next visit to the setting or in interviewing some of the people you saw there. In essence, you would be sampling from the possible settings, such as the day and time you observe and participants (people who seem to know what is going on) in order to understand what is important to know in the particular place you are studying.

7   Finally, evaluate your experience as a participant observer preparing field notes afterwards. How accurately were you able to recall the physical setting, events, and conversations? What strategies aided your recall? What will you do differently the next time you are in the field?

In-depth Interviewing

As we noted in an earlier chapter, an interview is a conversation with a purpose (Berg, 1989; Dexter, 1970; Lincoln and Guba, 1985). In qualitative studies, interviews often take place while one is a participant observer, although people in the setting may not realize that the informal conversations they have been engaged in are interviews. In the field it is sometimes possible to arrange interviews with people whom the researcher believes may add to her or his understanding of the phenomenon being studied. Formal arrangements such as this also take place when interviews are the primary means of inquiring about some phenomenon. Participants agree to be interviewed to help the researcher pursue his or her focus of inquiry.

In his book *Research Interviewing: Context and Narrative*, Elliot Mishler highlights the difference between a qualitative research interview and other standard forms of interviewing, and proposes a reformulation of the process:

> At its heart is the proposition that an interview is a form of discourse. Its particular features reflect the distinctive structure and aims of interviewing, namely, that it is discourse shaped and organized by asking and answering questions. An interview is a *joint product* of what interviewees and interviewers talk about together and how they talk with each other. The record of an interview that we researchers make and then use in our work of analysis and interpretation is a representation of that talk.
>
> (Mishler 1986: *vii*, italics added)

Qualitative studies that have employed Mishler's model of the research interview as the method of data collection have added substantially to our knowledge in many fields. In psychology, several important studies have illuminated important processes in women and men's intellectual development (Belenky *et al.*, 1986; Magolda, 1992; Perry, 1970), in adult identity development (Hancock, 1989; Whitbourne, 1986), in women's moral development (Gilligan, 1982), and in adolescence girls' psychological development (Brown and Gilligan, 1992). In education, in-depth interviewing has also been a fruitful method for better understanding children's educational experiences (Bogdan and Biklen, 1982), the lives of children and adults labeled *mentally retarded* (Bogdan and Taylor, 1975) and student life on college campuses (Kuh and Andreas, 1991). In cultural anthropology and sociology, the use of interviews to illuminate salient features of culture and human experience has a long and established history.

What characterizes the interviews presented in these research reports is the depth of the conversation, which moves beyond surface talk to a rich discussion of thoughts and feelings. Several features of the qualitative interviewing situation make this possible. First, qualitative interviews average one-and-a-half to two hours in length, allowing for *prolonged engagement* with the interviewee. This time frame allows the competent interviewer to establish rapport with the interviewee and to foster a climate of trust. Second, in many studies the interviewee is interviewed more than once, pursuing in subsequent interviews topics that emerge as important from preliminary data analysis. This kind of persistent involvement with interviewees makes it more likely that the researcher will come to understand at a deeper level their perceptions related to the phenomenon under study. Qualitative research interviews are typically referred to as *depth* or *in-depth* interviews (Lincoln and Guba, 1985; Taylor and Bogdan, 1984).

The skill of interviewing has been the subject of numerous books since it is a skill that has wide applicability. In our day-to-day interactions at home, work and school, and in fulfilling the requirements of jobs such as personnel officer, social worker, and program evaluator, we learn by asking others to inform us by answering our questions. The characteristics of a good qualitative interviewer are much the same as those that characterize people who are able to tactfully inquire and hear what others are saying. But perhaps most critical to being a skillful qualitative interviewer is deep and genuine curiosity about understanding another's experience.

For the purposes of qualitative research, the shape that an interview may take has been described in various ways. Common to most descriptions is a continuum of interview formats ranging from a structured format to a relatively unstructured format. The structure of the interview has to do primarily with the extent to which the questions to be asked of the interviewee are developed prior to the interview. Three main formats for an interview provide a useful beginning to a discussion on interviewing: the unstructured interview, the interview guide, and the interview schedule[1]. Each interview format differs in the level of skill required of the researcher to maintain the conversation around its purpose. Each format, however, shares a critical commonality: The questions are open-ended and designed to reveal what is important to understand about the phenomenon under study.

The Unstructured Interview[2]

Informal conversations initiated and guided by the researcher while in the field are a kind of unstructured interview. With one's focus of inquiry clearly in mind, the researcher tactfully asks and actively listens in order to understand what is important to know about the setting and the experiences of people in that setting. This purposeful conversation is not scripted ahead of time. Rather, the researcher asks questions pertinent to the study as opportunities arise, then listens closely to people's responses for clues as to what question to ask next, or whether it is important to probe for additional information. Jean Piaget (1926), an early pioneer of this method of inquiry, called it the *clinical method*. His focus of inquiry was to understand more about how children think.

Some qualitative researchers use the unstructured interview as their primary or only data collection method. Interviews are particularly important when one is interested in gaining *participant perspectives*, the language and meanings constructed by individuals (Bogdan and Biklen, 1982). The work of William Perry exemplifies this approach. Perry set out to investigate what is best summarized in the title of his research report, *Forms of Intellectual and Ethical Development in the College Years*. Perry invited a sample of male students attending Harvard University to volunteer to be interviewed about their college experience. The letter inviting participation read: 'We feel that students with different views about education may experience their years in college in very different ways and that it is vital to know about the different paths of this existence' (1970: 17). This invitation to be involved in the study was extended at the end of the men's freshman year. In his account of the research methodology, Perry (1970) describes the importance of providing an opportunity for students to share their own perceptions and terms with the interviewer, rather than having the interviewer influence students' responses through a more structured interview format. After several trials, Perry settled on the way to go about conducting the interview:

> We first welcomed the student, restated our interest in hearing from the students about their own experience, and asked permission (with assurance of anonymity) to [tape] record. We then said, in the general form developed by Merton (Merton, Fiske and Kendall, 1952): 'Why don't you start with whatever stands out for you about the year?'
>
> (Perry 1970: 19)

Using this single open-ended question and then relying on the skills of the interviewer to elaborate and extend the contents of each interview, Perry was able to make extraordinary use of the unstructured interview to understand male students' thinking. The epistemological theory that was derived from the Harvard students' interviews has paved the way for additional qualitative studies of adult thought and development (Belenky *et al.*, 1986; Gilligan, 1982).

The value of a single important question in framing a qualitative interview was evidenced in a study currently underway at a local middle school. The teachers and administrators were interested in understanding what school practices (including teaching practices) may be contributing to academic failure among students. The research team, made up of two university teacher-researchers and nine middle-school faculty members, set out to explore the perceptions of students, teachers and parents on this topic. After trying to develop an extensive set of open-ended questions to ask each of the constituency groups, the team came to the conclusion that one question captured the core of the inquiry: 'What school-based practices contribute to academic failure at this school?' Through relatively unstructured individual and group interviews the research team decided to pose this question as the basis for their study (Maykut and Erickson, 1992).[3]

Whether unstructured interviews are conducted in the field or arranged, the contents of the interviews must be written down. Informal interviews in the field are reconstructed and entered into the researcher's field notes. Arranged interviews are frequently audio tape-recorded, and if tape-recording is not desirable or possible, the researcher may take some notes during the interview and then reconstruct the interview afterwards. We will discuss note-taking during interviews and transcribing interviews from tape-recordings in a later section of this chapter.

The Interview Guide and Interview Schedule

It is quite possible that there is more than one key question that the researcher wants to pursue in a qualitative interview. A series of topics or broad interview questions which the researcher is free to explore and probe with the interviewee is usually referred to as an *interview guide* (Patton, 1990). An interview format consisting of a detailed set of questions and probes is called an *interview schedule*. In either situation, we have found the procedure illustrated in Figure 7.4 to be very helpful in developing an initial framework for the interview. In the actual interview situations, the skilled researcher will discover what is important to the interviewees, within the broad boundaries of the interview topics and questions, and pursue these new discoveries in the interview. Whether the researcher works alone or with a team, our procedure for developing a more structured interview guide has proven very useful. Team involvement in interview development can yield more interesting ideas than one might think of alone. We recommend that interview development work done with others be recorded as it happens

Figure 7.4: General procedure for developing an interview guide or an interview schedule

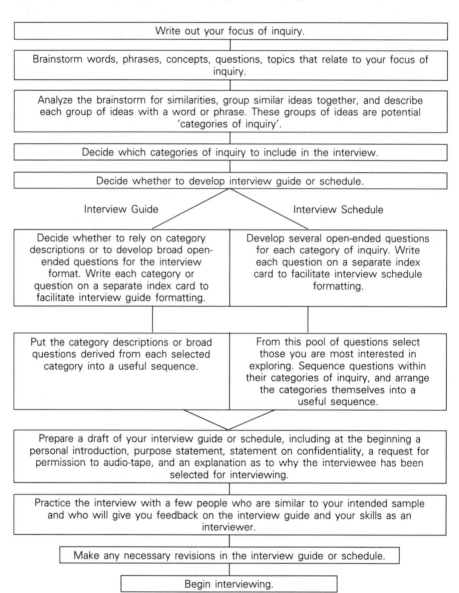

Write out your focus of inquiry.

Brainstorm words, phrases, concepts, questions, topics that relate to your focus of inquiry.

Analyze the brainstorm for similarities, group similar ideas together, and describe each group of ideas with a word or phrase. These groups of ideas are potential 'categories of inquiry'.

Decide which categories of inquiry to include in the interview.

Decide whether to develop interview guide or schedule.

Interview Guide   Interview Schedule

Decide whether to rely on category descriptions or to develop broad open-ended questions for the interview format. Write each category or question on a separate index card to facilitate interview guide formatting.

Develop several open-ended questions for each category of inquiry. Write each question on a separate index card to facilitate interview schedule formatting.

Put the category descriptions or broad questions derived from each selected category into a useful sequence.

From this pool of questions select those you are most interested in exploring. Sequence questions within their categories of inquiry, and arrange the categories themselves into a useful sequence.

Prepare a draft of your interview guide or schedule, including at the beginning a personal introduction, purpose statement, statement on confidentiality, a request for permission to audio-tape, and an explanation as to why the interviewee has been selected for interviewing.

Practice the interview with a few people who are similar to your intended sample and who will give you feedback on the interview guide and your skills as an interviewer.

Make any necessary revisions in the interview guide or schedule.

Begin interviewing.

on large pieces of easel or banner paper. Individual researchers will also benefit from putting their thinking on paper. This kind of graphic approach to interview development fosters idea-generating, synthesis and problem solving, and provides a reusable record of the individual or team's work (Sibbet, 1981). By maintaining a record of interview development, the researchers begin an 'audit trail' of their work, which contributes to the trustworthiness of the research outcomes (Lincoln and Guba, 1985).

Brainstorming

The first step in interview development is to write out the focus of inquiry. Recall from our earlier discussion that the focus of inquiry can be stated as a sentence or as a question. Next, we have found it useful to conduct a brainstorming session for the purpose of idea generation. The brainstorming session asks the researcher to freely consider what he or she might want to explore with people in order to understand the phenomenon being studied. Words, phrases, concepts, questions, and topics are quickly recorded without judging their worth to the inquiry. We suggest writing all over the paper, avoiding list-making that may restrict creative thinking (Rico, 1983; Sibbet, 1981). It is also useful to set a time limit for the brainstorming; approximately ten minutes is usually sufficient.

Developing categories of inquiry

Following a productive brainstorming session, the researcher usually has many ideas recorded. The next step toward interview development is to examine the ideas for similarities, and to group similar ideas together. This can be done directly on the brainstorming session paper by circling similar ideas with the same colored marker, or a new sheet of paper can be used to list similar ideas together. Next, develop a word or phrase that describes each cluster of ideas. We refer to these clusters of similar ideas as potential categories of inquiry for the interview. Note that the categories of inquiry are *inductively* derived from the working knowledge and ideas of the researcher. Finally, among your categories of inquiry select those which you are most interested in pursuing in the interview.

Deciding on a format

At this point the researcher needs to decide whether to develop an interview guide or a more elaborate interview schedule. There are several factors to consider in this decision: one's skill as an interviewer, one's working knowledge of the focus of inquiry, and whether the interviews are being conducted by more than one researcher. Beginning interviewers are more likely to find an interview guide providing too little direction for the interview. Supplementing an interview guide with possible questions, probes and cues can be quite useful, although a more structured interview schedule may be the better alternative. Experienced interviewers may like the freedom offered in the interview guide to ask questions and probe for information in their own way.

The interview guide format is especially suitable for exploring phenomena through interviewing when little is known about the topic. For example, we are currently conducting a qualitative study with two colleagues concerning the experience of US National Guard members who served in the Persian Gulf War in 1991 (Schafer, McClurg, Morehouse and Maykut, 1991). While Schafer and McClurg had considerable experience working with other war veterans, we had relatively little reliable information on men and women soldiers' experience in this recent war. We had the opportunity to conduct group interviews with interested soldiers during their first weekend of guard duty after the war. We developed the following interview guide to be used for the group interviews.

> *Desert storm interview guide: the experience of coming home*

- What is it like to be back together as a unit?
- What was it like to be in the [recent homecoming] parade?
  - •• What did you notice?
  - •• What did it feel like?
  - •• What did you hear?
- What surprises did you experience in coming home?
  - •• Were you surprised at anything *you* did?
  - •• Were you surprised at what other people did?
  - •• Did anything appear completely different to you upon returning?
    [Ask for specifics: How? What? When? Where?]
- What are some of the most important photos that you took while you were there?
- What pictures do you wish you had but do not?
- How do you feel about the way others behave or are responding to you?
- What's next for you?

Although we each had considerable skill in interviewing, we decided to co-conduct each group interview to allow us to more fully attend to the relatively large groups (13–23 people in each group). We began the group interview with the focus of our study: Understanding more about the experience of men and women who had served in the war, particularly that of coming home. There were brief introductions and then one of us asked the first question from the interview guide. The lively and far-ranging conversation that ensured, with our occasional requests for clarification, covered each of the questions in our guide, and more importantly, revealed many unexpected experiences and issues of importance among the veterans. The interview guide provided us with a framework for exploring experiences about which we were quite unfamiliar.

The decision to use an interview guide or an interview schedule is also influenced by the number of researchers involved in conducting interviews. When more than one researcher is involved it is often desirable to develop a more detailed interview format to ensure that interviewees are asked about the same topics (Lincoln and Guba, 1985; Patton, 1990). However, with skillful interviewing, unexpected topics are still allowed to emerge even out of the more structured interview schedule.

If the researcher chooses to develop an interview guide, the next decision is whether to simply list the categories of inquiry to be pursued in the interview or whether to pose a series of broad questions based on the categories of inquiry (see Figure 7.4). When using only the categories of inquiry, without prepared questions, the researcher must rely on her or his question-asking and other communication skills to conduct the interview. Many qualitative researchers prefer the openness of this approach. However, we strongly recommend some question preparation prior to any research interview, particularly for beginning researchers. In our study of Persian Gulf War veterans, we decided to pose several broad open-ended questions for our interview guide to help us articulate more clearly what we wanted to find out, and to provide some continuity across interviews conducted by different researchers.

Research exercise #10: Beginning the development of an interview

Examine the focus of inquiry that you developed in *Research exercise #6*. Would individual interviews with members of a relevant sample yield potentially useful information? If so, use this focus of inquiry for the exercises on interview development (#10–13). If your original focus of inquiry does not lend itself to interviewing as a means of data collection, develop a focus of inquiry that is better suited to interviewing. For this exercise we will be following the first few steps of the procedure for interview development outlined in Figure 7.4.

You will need several sheets of paper and pen or marker to complete this exercise.

1　The first step of this exercise returns us to the skills of brainstorming and concept mapping. On a plain sheet of paper, write your focus of inquiry in the center and circle it. A large piece of paper is helpful.
2　For the next five minutes, brainstorm words, phrases, concepts, questions and topics that you would like to pursue in an interview about your focus of inquiry. Write these words, concepts, etc., on the paper around your focus of inquiry, in the same way that you constructed a concept map for *Research exercise #5*.
3　Review the product of your brainstorming and cluster together similar ideas. Next, develop a word or phrase that describes each cluster. You can do this clustering by drawing in connections on your concept map, or by using a clean sheet of paper to record your work. These clusters are your *categories of inquiry* for developing interview questions. Review the categories of inquiry that you have developed and eliminate any categories that do not really interest you. Additional categories of inquiry can be added later as their importance becomes evident.
4　At this point it is useful to decide whether you want to develop an interview guide or a more structured interview schedule. Review the discussion above, *Deciding on a format*, to help you make your decision.

Preparing interview questions

As Stanley Payne (1951) noted, question-asking is an art, and like most art forms it is improved through practice and persistence. Whether the researcher is preparing questions for an interview guide or an interview schedule, there are many factors to consider. The primary consideration for qualitative research is that the questions be open-ended, inviting the interviewee to participate in a conversation. Open-ended questions often begin with the word such as, 'What do you think . . . ?' 'How do you feel . . . ?' 'In what way . . . ?' 'How might . . . ?' An open-ended question is one which is not easily answered with a discrete response, such as 'yes' or 'no', or a brief word or phrase. Questions that are designed to yield discrete responses of short answers are referred to as closed questions. They close down the conversation, and provide little opportunity for gaining participant perspectives. In order to conduct an interview that is experienced by both researcher and interviewee as 'a conversation with a purpose', it is essential to ask open-ended questions.

An example will help illustrate the difference between open and closed questions. In the dialogue below, a college teacher is trying to understand from a student how she might improve the second half of a semester-long course.

Question:　How do you think the course is going?
Answer:　　Fine, just fine.

Q: Have there been enough interesting classes to keep you coming to class?

A: Sure.

Q: What about the textbook? Do you find it worthwhile reading?

A: Yeah. It's not too bad.

Q: Do you think I require too many assignments or too few?

A: Definitely not too few!

Q: Do you think other students in the class share your views?

A: I think so.

Q: How would you grade your own work in the course so far?

A: Between a 'B' and 'C'.

Q: I've found your work very interesting to read. Thanks for the feedback on the class. See you Monday.

(Student thinks, 'That was quick.' Teacher thinks, 'Students just don't want to tell you what they really think.')

In the above example, the teacher asks the student a string of closed questions requiring little more than brief discrete responses. In normal conversation we often ask closed questions, while expecting and often getting the elaboration that is really implied in the question. In the above example, the teacher wants the student to tell her what it is *about* the course, the textbook, and the classes, what it is that makes the course 'OK'. This intention is lost on the student who simply responds to the questions as they are asked. The dialogue might have taken a different turn if the teacher had employed open-ended questions when talking with the student:

Q: I'm interested in knowing what students think about my teaching and course readings and assignments. Thinking back over the semester so far, how would you describe this course to others?

A: Hmm . . . Well, I would describe the course as usually quite interesting and involving. In lots of classes I just sit there, even if I have something to say. I don't know why, but I participate more in your class. Maybe it's because you have us do so many group things.

Q: Well, it is my intention to get students involved. We all tend to learn more that way. I'd like to ask you a little about the textbook. How do you go about reading a chapter and preparing for discussion in class?

A: (Pause) I started off reading it like I do other textbooks: a lot at one sitting and doing lots of highlighting. But that didn't really prepare me for the kind of questions you ask in class. And I didn't do too well on the first test, so I changed my way of reading. I'm reading it in smaller chunks and doing that thing you talked about in class. You know, where you write down questions you would like to ask the author if she were sitting right by me. It's helped a little, though sometimes it feels a sort of silly.

Q: I notice that you have done quite well on the class assignments. How do you manage that?

A: I found that to be pretty hard, because there are so many assignments. I've done OK so far, but as I look ahead at my schedule I don't know if I'll be able to keep it up.

Q: And what about the other students in the class? What do you think is the general opinion of the class regarding the number of assignments?

A: I can only speak for the group of students in the class I'm friends with. We are all concerned about the amount of work.

Q: I appreciate your candor. Your feedback has been very helpful. Thanks. See you Monday.

(Student thinks, 'I really had a chance to say what was on my mind, and I felt like she listened and cared about what I said. I also learned something about myself: I *like* to participate in class when the opportunities are there.' Teacher thinks, 'This is the kind of information I need to seek out more often. I'm getting a clear idea of what I might change and what I want to continue in the course.')

Given that the researcher seeks to develop open-ended questions, the task before him or her is to decide what questions to ask. We have the question typology presented by Patton (1990) to be useful as a guide to questions we might pose. Patton outlines six types of questions that may be asked in an interview:

- experience/behavior questions;
- opinion/value questions;
- feeling questions;
- knowledge questions;

- sensory questions; and
- background/demographic questions.

Experience/behavior questions ask about what people do or have done, such as 'What kinds of things do you do on this job?' Experience/ behavior questions are quite useful to begin an interview, particularly when they ask people to describe what they are currently doing. This is clearly something the interviewee knows about and can offer to begin the conversation.

Patton makes a useful distinction between opinion/value questions and feeling questions. The former tap into beliefs which are primarily cognitive in nature, such as, 'What do you think about the company's new leave policy?' or 'What is your opinion about renegotiating the new contract?' In contrast, feeling questions ask about affective states, such as, 'What kinds of feelings did you experience when you heard about the plant closing?' Interviewers should be clear about what kind of information they are seeking — thoughts or feelings — and provide appropriate questions and cues to the interviewees.

Knowledge questions ask interviewees to tell what they know about a particular topic, tapping into their factual knowledge, such as 'What is contained in the company's position description for this job?' or 'What is the procedure at your office for filing a sexual harassment complaint?' This type of question can be especially threatening if interviewees believe they should know the answer and do not. Interviews can be derailed if the interviewees begin to see the session as a grilling on topics for which they cannot supply the necessary information.

Sensory questions are designed to tap into what the interviewee sees, hears, touches, smells and tastes, and can provide the researcher with a kind of vicarious experience. The interviewee may be able to let interviewer 'stand in his shoes' by descriptively responding to such questions as, 'What do you notice first when you walk onto the stage?' or 'What does the psychologist say to you when you enter his office?'

Background/demographic questions may be important in helping the researcher characterize each interviewee, as well as the sample that eventually comprises the study. Sociodemographic information should not, however, be gathered ambiguously it is routinely gathered in other types of research. These questions should be asked if they are potentially useful to understand the phenomenon under study. If included, information such as age, years of experience, marital status, residence, etc., which is factual, brief, and sometimes perceived as quite intrusive, is usually best gathered at the end of the interview. Occasionally, the interviewer may have the opportunity to gather background information unobtrusively at various points in the interview. For example: 'So, you've been at this job for five years. How old were you when you started here?' allows this interviewer to calculate the person's current age without asking directly.

Another feature of Patton's question typology is the time frame of each question. A question can be posed in the present, past, or future tense. The types of questions asked and the time frame reflected by each question will be broadly determined by the researcher's focus of inquiry.

Patton's question typology provides a useful place to start developing a few broad questions for an interview guide or for formulating the many questions that comprise an interview schedule. Patton's typology is especially useful for the latter. But before you prepare an interview guide or schedule, it is helpful to practice developing interview questions.

Research exercise #11: Developing interview questions

Your work in the previous exercise will prepare you for this practice activity. Whether or not you have decided to develop an interview guide or an interview schedule, use your focus of inquiry and categories of inquiry from *Research exercise #10* for this activity.

You will need several sheets of paper (or index cards) and pen or marker to complete this exercise.

1   Your categories of inquiry now serve as the framework for developing interview questions. To gain practice in preparing questions, try to develop an example (or two!) of each type of question Patton (1990) identifies: a) experience/behavior questions; b) opinion/value questions; c) feeling questions; d) knowledge questions; e) sensory questions; and f) background/demographic questions. To begin, select any one of your categories of inquiry and develop an experience/behavior question; then develop other types of questions for this same category of inquiry. Or, use other categories of inquiry as the basis for developing various types of questions. The point is to expand your skill at developing useful interview questions, so prepare several different questions. We recommend writing each question on a separate sheet of paper or index card for later use. Also indicate the type of question you have asked, using Patton's typology. The format illustrated below is helpful in organizing the many features of interview question development. The example shown was part of the pool of possible questions developed by students for a study exploring the experiences and perspectives of high-achieving college students (Anderson *et al.*, 1991).

    - Category of inquiry: *Approaches to learning inside the classroom*
    - Interview question: *If I was in the same classes with you, what would I see you doing during a lecture?*
    - Type of question (experience/behavior, opinion/value, feeling, knowledge, sensory, demographic): *experience/behavior*
    - Time frame of question (past, present, or future): *present*

2   Review each of your practice questions and determine the time frame indicated by each question: past, present or future. Write down the time frame of each question on your paper.

Good interview questions, ones that will draw the research participant into conversation and yield useful information, can be challenging to develop. There are three major pitfalls that beginning researchers encounter in developing questions for a research interview: the closed question, the unclear or vague question and the complex question. The closed question sometimes appears as a multiple-choice question, requiring the participant to respond to an implied response set. The question, 'To what extent does this academic program meet your needs?' is a closed question, directing the individual to reply in some variation of the following: a) to a large extent; b) to some extent; or c) not at all. Another type of closed question identified by Patton is the dichotomous question, one whose wording suggests that a 'yes' or 'no' response is desired, such as 'Were you satisfied with the academic supports provided by the school's learning center?' Closed questions can cut off conversation unless they are followed by related questions or probes. It is advisable practice to try to open up the question rather than to rely heavily on the use of follow-up questions or probes.

Interview questions that are unclear or vague are likely to result if the intent of the research study is unclear to the researcher. A clear focus of inquiry is essential for both preplanned and on-the-spot opportunities to gather information. In addition, trying out questions with interested others and asking for frank feedback will help you fine-tune the clarity of your questions.

The third major pitfall in developing interview questions is making them too complex. Each interview question should be one singular question, not a string of embedded questions that the participant has to hold in his or her mind. The question, 'How did you go about solving that problem, and how did you feel about the outcome?' is a complex question, easily divided into two questions. Your research participants will appreciate your simplicity.

Review the interview questions you developed for *Research exercise #12*. Do your questions relate to your focus of inquiry? Have you clearly identified the type of questions you have developed, using Patton's typology? Have you identified the time frame of each question: past, present or future? Are each of your questions open-ended? Is the meaning of each question clear? Is each question a singular question? In qualitative interviewing the wording of the questions affects the kind of responses the research participant gives and the richness and quality of the interview itself.

Drafting the interview guide or interview schedule

In our discussion of interview development, we have examined several important steps: developing a focus of inquiry; brainstorming and refining categories of inquiry; deciding on a format, either an interview guide or a schedule; and preparing interview questions. With practice developing interview questions, you probably have a better idea about which interview format you would choose if you were actually going to pursue your focus of inquiry. If we return to the procedural diagram outlining interview development (see Figure 7.4), we see that the decision to prepare an interview guide means you will either use your categories of inquiry as your guide for the interview, or you will develop a small set of broad open-ended questions, based on your categories of inquiry. If you choose to develop an interview schedule, you will need to develop a larger set of open-ended interview questions, and organize them into a useful sequence. As we indicated above, it is especially helpful to write out each potential question on a separate sheet of paper or index card. Each question in your pool of possible questions can then be easily omitted or added, and selected questions can be easily sequenced within categories of inquiry. Categories of inquiry themselves can then be put in a reasonable order for the interview.

Although there is no single best way to sequence questions in an interview schedule, Patton (1990) again offers some useful suggestions. One, begin the interview with noncontroversial questions framed in the present, focusing on the interviewee's experiences or behaviors. Two, save potentially threatening knowledge questions until some rapport has been established with the interviewee. Three, minimize the number of background and demographic questions, and intersperse them throughout the interview, as appropriate. Careful attention to the ordering of questions will increase the likelihood of a productive interview. However, in the process of conducting a research interview there is no substitute for knowing your interview questions well. The sequence of questions is really set by the interviewee, and it is the qualitative interviewer's job to be alert and responsive, to sense an opportune time to ask a question, and to know when a question has been answered out of sequence.

In preparing a draft of the interview guide or an interview schedule, it is important to begin the interview with several important features: *a personal introduction; a statement of purpose*, including what will be done with the results of the study; a statement indicating the *confidentiality* of the interview; a statement regarding *note-taking* that may take place during the interview; a request for *permission to audiotape record* the interview, should taping be possible; and a statement *informing the interviewee* why he or she is being interviewed. Two interview schedules are included in the Appendix. The first interview schedule was developed to understand more about the role of television among college students. The second interview schedule was designed to explore young adults' experience with cross-sex friendships in a joint interview conducted with pairs of friends. We chose the interview schedule format because several student researchers were involved in each study.

It is possible to combine the features of an interview guide with an interview schedule to suit the purposes of the study. The interview schedules that appear in the Appendix are highly structured, providing the questions to be asked, possible probes, and additional directions to the interviewer. Both interview schedules were designed in large part by undergraduate students in our qualitative research course. These students come into the course with different levels of interviewing experience and expertise, and a structured interview schedule allows beginners to fully participate on a research team. Student researchers can choose to restate questions in their own words, vary the order of topics in order to be responsive to the interviewee, and explore and probe topics broadly related to the focus of inquiry.

Using probes in qualitative research interviews

An important skill for qualitative researchers is the use of probes or follow-up questions in a research interview. For more information on probes, we turn again to Patton's work. He defines a probe as 'an interview tool used to go deeper into the interview responses' (1990: 238). Since the purpose of the qualitative research interview is to gain a deep understanding of the interviewee's experience and perspective, using probes effectively is an important qualitative research skill. By probing an interviewee's response, we are likely to add to the richness of the data, and end up with a better understanding of the phenomenon we are studying.

Patton (1990) identifies three types of probes: detail-oriented probes, elaboration probes, and clarification probes. These probes are not usually written into an interview guide or schedule; they are held in the interviewer's 'back pocket' and used as the need arises.

1. *Detail-oriented probes.* In our natural conversations we ask each other questions to get more detail. These types of follow-up questions are designed to fill out the picture of whatever it is we are trying to understand. We easily ask these questions when we are genuinely curious.

- Who was with you?
- What was it like being there?
- Where did you go then?

- When did this happen in your life?
- How are you going to try to deal with the situation?

2. *Elaboration probes*. Another type of probe is designed to encourage the interviewee to tell us more. We indicate our desire to know more by such things as gently nodding our head as the person talks, softly voicing 'un-huh' every so often, and sometimes by just remaining silent but attentive. We can also ask for the interviewee to simply continue talking.

- Tell me more about that.
- Can you give me an example of what you are talking about?
- I think I understand what you mean.
- Talk more about that, will you?
- I'd like to hear you talk more about that.
- That's helpful. Can you talk a little more about that?

3. *Clarification probes*. There are likely to be times in an interview when the interviewer is unsure of what the interviewee is talking about, what she or he means. In these situations the interviewer can gently ask for clarification, making sure to communicate that it is the interviewer's difficulty in understanding and not the fault of the interviewee.

- I'm not sure I understand what you mean by 'hanging out'. Can you help me understand what that means?
- I'm having trouble understanding the problem you've described. Can you talk a little more about that?
- I want to make sure I understand what you mean. Would you describe it for me again?
- I'm sorry. I don't quite get. Tell me again, would you?

You can become skillful at using probes by becoming aware of your use of them in day-to-day conversation and also by practicing using them in more formal situations. Tape-recording interviews and replaying them to examine your use of probes is a helpful skill-building technique. Simply rehearsing different probes that you can use in an actual interview can be extremely helpful. You might also want to pencil in possible probes on your interview guide or schedule that you could use in the actual interview.

A note on structure

In qualitative research a structured interview does not replace the human as the instrument of the study. The qualitative posture is one of flexibility and responsiveness to the expected emergence of unanticipated twists and turns in the content of the interview. It is quite possible that once the interview is begun, it becomes clear that what is important to pursue about the phenomenon under study is not reflected in the prepared questions. The human instrument expects the unexpected and adapts and probes the salient aspects with the interviewee. As these new aspects are revealed to the researcher, she or he refocuses the inquiry and subsequent interviews. In Patton's words, 'The fundamental principle of qualitative interviewing is to provide a framework within which the respondents can express their own understandings in their own terms' (1990: 290). The contrast between the emergent design of qualitative studies and the fixed a priori design of traditional quantitative studies is striking.

Research exercise #12: Drafting an interview guide or an interview schedule

This exercise builds on the work you did for the two previous exercises. If you completed these exercises you have in hand a focus of inquiry, several categories of inquiry, and several practice interview questions. You may or may not be able to use your practice questions for this exercise (be willing to give them up!). Look through your categories of inquiry and select those you are most interested in pursuing in an interview. Now you are ready to draft either an interview guide (see Part A below) or an interview schedule (see Part B below). Keep in mind that the qualitative research interview is an attempt to conduct an in-depth interview, designed to last one-and-a-half to two hours. The content and number of questions should be designed accordingly.

Part A: Drafting an interview guide. Recall that an interview guide is comprised of a relatively short set of topics (categories of inquiry) or a short set of broad open-ended questions. For this exercise, we suggest you develop a short set of questions for your guide. Select four to six categories of inquiry on which to base your interview questions. For each selected category of inquiry, develop one or two broad open-ended questions. Then sequence all the questions, taking into consideration the information provided above on sequencing, and your own sense of the possible. Be sure to include a personal introduction, a statement of purpose, assurances of confidentiality, etc., at the beginning of your interview guide. Draft a complete interview guide.

Part B: Drafting an interview schedule. An interview schedule is comprised of many carefully constructed questions, follow-up questions or probes, and possibly other information for the interviewer. It is substantially longer than an interview guide and is an especially useful method of data collection for beginning researchers and research teams, to achieve some consistency in the topics of information pursued. For this exercise, select several categories of inquiry on which to base your interview questions. These categories will provide an overall framework for your interview schedule. For each selected category, develop several open-ended questions. Depending on your focus of inquiry, these questions may cover some or all of the types of interview questions described by Patton (1990) and one or all three time frames. It is helpful to prepare a large pool of possible questions from which to select the most promising ones for the interview schedule. Once you have selected the best questions, sequence them within their respective categories of inquiry, and sequence the categories themselves. You may need to eliminate some questions or categories of the interview because of its unwieldy length. Recall that you are trying to design an interview that will last about one-and-a-half to two hours. After you have settled on the final items, be sure to add a personal introduction, a statement of purpose, assurances of confidentiality, etc., at the beginning. Prepare a complete draft of your interview schedule.

Refining the interview format

After developing the complete draft of an interview, particularly if several questions are being asked, it is helpful to practice the interview with a few people who are similar to the people who will make up the research sample. It is quite beneficial to practice the interview with people who will provide constructive feedback on the contents and format of the interview itself and on your skills as an interviewer. Necessary changes can be made in the interview format and content, and you can identify interviewing skills that need further development.

Interviewing equipment

Qualitative researchers have taken quite extreme positions on whether it is appropriate to audio-tape record an interview, ranging from 'not tape recording unless there are legal or training reasons for doing so' (Lincoln and Guba, 1985: 272), to valuing the tape recorder as 'part of the indispensable equipment' of the qualitative interviewer (Patton, 1990: 348). We are in agreement with Patton on the importance of tape recording whenever allowable to obtain the best possible record of the interviewee's words. Tape-recording is essential if one plans to use interviews as the main source of data. In most cases, the presence of the tape recorder quickly fades to the background, particularly if the interviewer is adept at using the machine and the participants in the interview are engaged in the experience.

Conducting the interview

The responsibility for establishing and maintaining a positive interviewing climate rests with the interviewer. Moreover, 'the quality of the information obtained during an interview is largely dependent on the interviewer' (Patton, 1990: 279). An interviewer who knows his or her questions well, who listens more than talks, and who is genuinely curious about the the topic and what the interviewee has to say about it will maximize the chances of a good interview. More importantly, an interviewer who communicates, through words and behaviors, that the interviewee is a *collaborator* in the research process begins to reduce the power differential between the two. According to Mishler, this kind of empowerment in the interviewer–interviewee relationship can assist people in 'their efforts to construct coherent and reasonable worlds of meaning and to make sense of their experiences' (1986: 118). When the balance of power is shifted, notes Mishler, interviewees are more likely to tell their own stories.

A prepared and curious interviewer committed to involving his or her interviewees as research collaborators is still likely to need some help with the logistics of the research interview. The following set of guidelines can help organize the interviewing experience and ensure a complete transcript:

1 Gather together the materials and equipment you will need to conduct the interview, including tape recorder (batteries, electrical cord, extension cord), cassette tapes, interview guide, and pen and paper for note taking. It is helpful to gather these materials together into a data collection kit for this and future interviews.

2 Meet your interviewee promptly at the scheduled time and place. Note whether there is potential background noise that might interfere with a clear recording. Test the tape recorder with the interviewee, replay your test comments, and suggest adjustments, such as speaking more loudly, if necessary. Conduct the interview.

3 Immediately after you have completed the interview, reflect on the interview in writing. The interviewer's notes prepared following the interview are part of your data. Write down the things that the tape recorder did not capture, such as facial expressions, body posture, mood, and any other observations that can contribute to making sense of the interviewee's perspective. Here is a short excerpt from an interviewer's notes written after a joint in-depth interview with a pair of opposite-sex friends:

> Throughout the interview Ellie and Dan maintained a great deal of eye contact. They appeared very interested in each other's responses, maintaining their attention on each other. This interest was particularly intense when they talked a few times about their romantic attraction to one another at different times in their friendship. As they stated in the interview, some of the details of this attraction were new to each of them.

> It is also a good idea to record your own feelings during the interview, to keep in front of you how you may have

influenced what was conveyed during the session. For example, when might you have been leading? Talking too much? Cutting off the interviewee? Really 'clicking'? Also, write down your insights, hunches, ideas, questions, etc., that relate to the focus of inquiry. Reflect on what you are learning that can help focus your subsequent data collection efforts. Write these notes down right away!

We strongly suggest avoiding conversation about the interview until after you have transcribed it. Then, if you do talk to anyone about it afterwards, be sure to adhere to the confidentiality agreement.

Guidelines for Transcribing Interviews

Preparing a complete transcript from an audio-taped interview is especially important when interviews are a main source of data for a qualitative study. This is a time-consuming and demanding task. For a one-and-a-half to two hour interview, you should plan on at least twenty hours of transcribing, although this will vary depending upon the length of the interview and whether you print or type the transcript. We strongly recommend transcribing an interview soon after it has occurred, while it is still fresh in the researcher's mind. The process of timely transcription often reminds the researcher of important behaviors that were not captured by the tape recorder.

It is preferable to type the interview transcript using a word processing program on a microcomputer. Headphones and an on-off pedal for the tape recorder speed the process considerably. Computer-stored work allows for easy editing, a backup copy, and easily made multiple copies on a computer printer. Typed copy makes analysis much easier, particularly when working with a research team. However, for beginning researchers, if typing presents a significant hardship, it is possible to very clearly print the transcript in dark ink. Whether you type or print, we suggest following these guidelines for clarity and greater ease during data analysis:

- use only one side of the paper
- use clean-edged paper to facilitate photocopying
- use a dark ribbon or pen
- use 1 1/2 inch margins on all sides of the paper
- single-space when the same person is speaking
- double-space between speakers
- double-space between paragraphs of the same speaker

There are several important items of information to include at the beginning of the interview transcript. Begin the transcript noting the pseudonym you have given to the person you interviewed and the initial you will use in the transcript to indicate when your interviewee is speaking. An excerpt from an interview with a man in our study of the lives of older adults is shown in Figure 7.5 (Maykut *et al.*, 1992). In the transcript the student researcher indicates that *Ben* is the interviewee's pseudonym, and a *B* will be used to show when Ben is speaking. The first page of the transcript should also include the interviewer's name and the initial that will be used when he is speaking, the date of the interview, the time when it occurred (start and finish) and where it took place.

In the upper right-hand corner of every page of the transcript, it is important to indicate the type of data contained in the manuscript; in this case it is a transcript (T), as compared to observations (O) from the field. Next to the type of data, the researcher puts the interviewee's initial and the page number of the transcript. In the example in Figure 7.5, the code in the top right-hand corner, T/B-1, indicates that this is the first page of the transcript of the interview with *Ben*.

The record of the interview itself is preceded by a brief paragraph that sets the stage for the interview: a description of the physical setting, a description of the interviewee, and a description of how the researcher came to interview this person, for example, arranged through a mutual friend.

Words are the data of qualitative research, and it is important to carefully and completely transcribe the audio-taped interview. Although many qualitative researchers have their interviews transcribed for them, preparing one's own transcripts provides an important opportunity to relive the interview and become substantially more familiar with the data. We recommend writing down everything that has been recorded on the tape. No short-cuts. Start a new line for each speaker and indicate by initial who is speaking. When the interviewee is talking for long segments of time, break the monologue into paragraphs. Start new paragraphs often, as ideas change. You do not, however, have to transcribe every 'umm' and 'ah'! It is sufficient to note the first 'um' or 'ah' in a series, and then proceed to the words.

There are a few other well-established conventions for transcribing that are helpful to use. As noted above, brackets indicate an addition to the recorded interview by the researcher. In the transcript example shown in Figure 7.5, the student researcher has used brackets to set apart his own commentary from the recorded words. His additions are intended to improve understanding, such as clarifying the places the

Figure 7.5: An excerpt from the transcript of an in-depth interview conducted by a student researcher

Pseudonym for interviewee: *Ben (B)*
Cities and other places described in the interview have been changed in the transcript in order to protect the identity of the interviewee.
Name of interviewer: *Jeff (J)*
Date of interview: 4/31/92
Time: 2:45–4:00 pm
Setting: Ben's home

Ben is a retired priest affiliated with the diocese of Cedar Rapids, Iowa. Ben is 74-years-old. The interview took place in Ben's home located on the northern edge of the city. We were sitting in his living room with the tape recorder located between us on the coffee table. A mutual friend, who is also a priest, asked Ben if he would be interested in doing an interview with me. He agreed.

J: Ben, do I have your permission to tape record this interview?

B: Yes, you have my approval. You can record the interview.

J: O.K. Ah, to start out I'd like you to tell me a little bit about how long you've lived here and what brought you to this area.

B: Are you talking about the area here in Iowa?

J: Yes.

B: I came to Iowa in 1950, in December, so I've been here ever since.

J: Was that due to your work, or just —

B: I became incardinated in the diocese later, but you have to be out three years, so I came here and I first went to, ah, St. Thomas Moore parish, with Father Alfred Engler. And I was there a short time and then was transferred to Blessed Sacrament [parish]. And at that time I taught at Cathedral [high school], religion.

J: I went to Cathedral for high school.

B: Did you really?

J: Yes.

B: Well, I taught there from Blessed Sacrament, and then I was transferred to St. Patrick's [St. Patrick's parish in Cedar Rapids], and I was there for six years, and taught part-time at Cathedral for awhile, two or three years.

J: Um, so how do you spend your free time now then? Well, what do you do every day, your daily routine, things like that?

B: [laughing] Well, I have — If I'm home I have mass. I set up an alter right there [pointing to a counter in the kitchen] — it's on the counter. I have mass intentions, but actually at least three or four times a week I am saying mass elsewhere right now, either at St. Catherine Convent, sometimes there, especially on Sundays, and at St. Peter's Hospital. /?/ Either during Lent or noon mass or the 3:15 pm mass. I'm on call quite often because they're down to one priest now — they used to have two, Father Simolski and Father John. Now they're down to Father John so they have to get someone to fill in. So you are on call for eight hours at a time and very often they'll join to that one or two masses, or they will have mass at the St. Catherine Home, which is joined to them, or the home on Gardner Street. So I can say mass there very often. So, about three or four times a week I am busy saying mass elsewhere.

J: So you keep pretty busy?

B: Right. That's just the mass part. [I laugh a little.]

J: So, on your free time, do you have any hobbies or interests you pursue?

B: Well [laughs], I cut fire wood, mow the lawn, try to do anything I can around here. My hobby used to be fishing until I moved right down next to the lake. Now I don't do much fishing anymore, right here.

interviewee, *Ben*, is referring to by certain proper nouns. This bracketing of the researcher's comments is the same procedure used in field notes to separate the researcher's observations from his or her commentary (see Figure 7.1).

For various reasons, words or phrases in an audio-taped interview sometimes cannot be deciphered. In these instances it is acceptable to print: /?/. Other useful conventions: A dash following a word indicates that the speaker cut off the word or phrase, which often is a parenthetical comment or a false start. Three unspaced periods indicate a pause (...). Three spaced periods show that several lines have been omitted (. . .). *Italics* indicate emphatic stress. In a recent study we interviewed pairs of opposite-sex friends who sometimes overlapped each other's statements. We have indicated overlap by using vertical lines:

Female: There are some things that I don't tell | Nick about.
Male: | What do you
mean? I thought we could talk to each other about everything. Now you tell me you can't.

When you have completed the transcript, make a complete photocopy. Many qualitative researchers recommend the practice of providing the interviewee with a draft of the transcript so that corrections can be made if necessary. The goal here is not to transform the interview from normal conversation, with its usual dysfluencies, but to clearly understand the meaning the interviewee was trying to convey. Most interviewees appreciate the importance given to their interview. Field notes from participant observations are also typed using the general format outlined above, such as initialing each page, using 1 1/2 inch margins on all sides, etc.

Group Interviews

For student-researchers as well as for ourselves, group interviews have often presented us with the unexpected — unexpected interactions, insights, ideas, and information. But perhaps this is what we should have expected! As researcher David Morgan (1988) emphasizes, the purpose of doing a group interview is to bring several different perspectives into contact. It is the very nature of the group experience that sets this method of qualitative data collection apart from the others. However, like individual interviewing and participant observation, the purpose of conducting a group interview is to understand what people experience and perceive about the focus of inquiry, through a process that is open and emergent.

Before we discuss interviewing in groups, we want to note that there are particular situations where the most appropriate group to be interviewed may consist of only two people. These 'conjoint interviews' have been used successfully in some recent qualitative family research studies (Gilgun, Daly and Handel, 1992). In one study, Kerry Daly (1992) explored the experiences of infertile couples at various stages of their consideration of adoptive parenthood through the use of conjoint interviews. Daly notes that while couples may collude to protect their private behaviors or inadvertently disclose information that violates the privacy rights of the other, the advantages of conjoint interviewing outweigh the disadvantages. She and other researchers argue that interviewing couples generates a more accurate picture of family life (Bennett and McAvity, 1985; Daly, 1992). Other topic areas, such as teachers' experience of team-teaching or the experiences of best-friend dyads may be best explored through this two-person variation of the group interview.

We define a group interview as *a group conversation with a purpose*. The qualitative researcher brings together a relatively small group of people, typically six to eight, to find out what they think, feel, or know about the researcher's focus of inquiry. It is important, however, to distinguish the group interview used in qualitative research from another situation that is sometimes referred to as a group interview; that is, a set of individual interviews that take place in a group setting. While the latter may be convenient and efficient, using the group setting in this way does not take advantage of the most important quality of the group interview: using the dynamics of group interaction to gain information and insights that are less likely to be gained through individual interviews or participant observation. Some researchers have preferred to use the term *focus group* to refer to the group interview that emphasizes dynamic group interactions, among other things (Krueger, 1988; Morgan, 1988).[4]

The group interview occupies an important place in qualitative research, combining some of the features of individual interviewing and participant observation. In essence, the group interview is an opportunity to observe a selected group of people discussing the topic that most interests the researcher. In naturalistic observations, the participant observer may not be lucky enough to hear and see a discussion of her or his research questions. In the informal but somewhat unnatural setting of the group interview, the chance to do so is created.

In a well-conducted group interview, participants have an opportunity to listen to each other's contributions, which may spark new insights or help them develop their ideas more clearly. Information that may not be thought of or shared in the individual interview may emerge in the group process. People often enjoy and learn about themselves from participating in a group interview. They have an opportunity to think aloud about their private perceptions of issues or events, sometimes coming to new understanding through their interactions with others in the group. Researchers are sometimes able to 'see' people thinking through these interactions and can gain fresh insight into how people construct their worlds. Morgan (1988) believes group interviews are especially useful for investigating what people think and for uncovering why people think as they do.

Group interviews are also useful for helping the researcher explore a topic that is new to him or her, or for which little information is available. The information and ideas that can potentially be generated through group discussion can provide the researcher with important research questions to pursue in other groups and/or with other methods of data collection. Thus the group interview can be an efficient means of helping the researcher begin to focus on the more salient aspects of the phenomenon under study.

Yet another benefit of the group interview is to provide participants with the opportunity to check out the researcher. If the researcher is pursuing an area of inquiry that is especially personal or likely to yield socially desirable responses, the group interview provides the researcher with a chance to demonstrate his or her sensitivity to the views and experiences of the research participants. This is particularly valuable if the researcher wants to conduct individual follow-up interviews with the group members, in which case being a nonjudgmental and trustworthy interviewer are crucial.

Planning the Group Interview

There are two main considerations in planning a group interview(s) as part of qualitative data collection: Who should I include in the group? and What should I ask them? Clearly, the researcher's focus of inquiry will provide some initial direction for answering these questions.

The group as a small sample

It is helpful to think of the potential members of the group interview as a small sample. Within this small sample you will want to include people who are, of course, relevant to your study. If you are interested in exploring teenager's experiences with dating in the 1990s, you will want to compose your group of teenagers. But beyond this general sampling category you will have to decide, or 'hunch', which factors or variables contribute to differences in dating experience likely to be found among teenagers. Previous research may provide some clues, particularly if the research is qualitative. Note here that we are applying the concept of 'maximum variation' to building the sample for the group interview. (See the earlier section on Building a Sample for a more detailed discussion of sampling and maximum variation.)

Based on your initial hunches about what contributes to variability in the experience of dating (or some other topic of study), you can begin to build profiles of potential group interview members. In our example, we can speculate that gender, age, and school culture are likely to be important to understanding the dating experience. With this in mind we would begin to recruit participants for the group interview, seeking out girls and boys of different teen ages, and from different schools. We might further decide that young teens and older teens may not be a good combination for the dynamics of the group interview, given their different experiences in middle school and high school, and decide to make the groups more homogeneous. Likewise, we might speculate that same-sex groups are likely to yield more truthful information, i.e., less influenced by what the other-sex members of the group will think about one's experience and perspectives. As you can see, the types of decisions one makes about group composition are intimately tied to the researcher's focus of inquiry and knowledge about the topic.

How many people should be in a group interview? Again, there are a few things to consider. There no single best number, but the outside limits appear to be no fewer than four and generally no more than twelve (Krueger, 1988; Morgan, 1988). In our group interview with Desert Storm War veterans, described earlier, we had no idea how many veterans would volunteer to participate in our group interviews on the day we were invited to their weekend training duty. We ended up with groups that ranged from 13 to 24 members, and we were still able to have 'a group conversation with a purpose'. However, we highly recommend (a) smaller groups that are more likely to ensure that everyone will be able to be part of the discussion, and (b) large enough groups that will contribute to diversity in perspective.

How long should the interview be? If we think about the things that need to be accomplished in the interview, it becomes clear why the group interview needs to be at least an hour, possibly two hours in length. Most participants will want to get acquainted with other group members and the researcher before they are willing to share their private experiences and perspectives. This trust-building takes some prolonged engagement. It is best to schedule a group interview for two hours, and plan for a one-and-a-half hour group interview. A two-hour block will provide sufficient flexibility should the interview be shorter or longer in length.

There are several logistical considerations in conducting group interviews. Obviously, you need to be able to arrange a time for the interview when everyone invited can attend. The setting for the interview should be comfortable and quiet. Tape recording equipment must be ready and working. You will also want to have a pen and paper ready to record notes, such as where people are sitting, questions to come back to, etc. Now, what will you ask in the interview?

Preparing the group interview guide

An interview guide is often a useful tool for the researcher to use in the group interviewing situation (Patton, 1990). Recall that an interview guide is a relatively brief series of topics or questions the researcher uses to guide the group's conversation. Recommendations vary on how many topics or questions comprise a useful interview guide, but most researchers agree that it is important to have at least two broadly stated topics or questions, with possible subtopics and probes ready. We have typically developed four to six questions or topics for use in group interviews. An example of an interview guide prepared by a student researcher is shown in Figure 7.6. The focus of inquiry for this student's study was to understand how college students define prejudice and how they interpret their own prejudicial behavior. The student researcher chose to begin her study with a group interview in order to explore the possibilities for studying self-perceptions of prejudice through interviews, and to identify potentially salient topics for individual follow-up interviews.

It is tempting for beginning researchers to build an extensive interview guide that resembles an interview schedule. While this kind of preparation can help ease the anxiety of conducting group interviews, a highly structured interview schedule will stifle conversation, especially if the researcher is determined to cover all the questions and involve all the participants. Like other research skills, practice in conducting group interviews will hone the researcher's ability to ask a few broad open-ended questions to generally focus the discussion and then probe for further information and ideas. It is in the interviewing situation that the human-as-instrument is most tested.

Figure 7.6: Group interview guide developed by a student researcher for a qualitative study of prejudice among college students

Group Interview Guide
- Welcome.
- Individual approval for audio-taping the interview.
  - •• Permission to record the interview on tape.
  - •• Confirmation of confidentiality agreement; participants understand that their names will not be used in any way, nor will information be shared that reveals their identity in any way.
  - •• Inform participants that any time during the interview the tape recorder can be turned off.
- Introductions
  - •• Familiarize everyone.
  - •• What made you decide to participate in this group?
- Opening Question
  - •• What kinds of things are on your mind about this subject, *prejudice*?
- Questions
  - •• How do you define prejudice? [Develop a group definition of prejudice and record on large paper for all group members to see.*]
  - •• What are some situations where you have been aware of prejudice? Preface questions with phrases like, 'I understand we all want to be good people . . .', or, 'I understand it might be a little uncomfortable to talk about, but . . .']
    - ••• What were you thinking at the time?
    - ••• Have you ever been aware of yourself having a prejudice?
    - ••• What are some of the ways people maintain prejudice in society?
    - ••• How do we prevent change?
    - ••• Discuss participants perspectives about current events.
    - ••• School newspaper's recent articles on prejudice. [bring copies]
    - ••• Ku Klux Klan events in Iowa and throughout country.
    - ••• College campus regulations that restrict harassing or intimidating language.
- End
  - •• Fill out brief profile of own educational background, rural or urban hometown, and religious background. Indicate interest in a follow-up interview.
  - •• Reconfirm confidentiality agreement.
  - •• Thank you for participating.

For reference: Webster's dictionary definition of *prejudice*: preconceived judgment or opinion; an adverse opinion or leaning formed without just grounds or before sufficient knowledge; an irrational attitude of hostility directed against an individual, a group, a race, or their supposed characteristics.

Conducting the Group Interview

The fact that group interviews bring together several participants for an open conversation around a specific topic means that the researcher will have a less prominent role than in the one-to-one individual interviewing situation. The researcher's role in the group interview has sometimes been characterized as *moderator*, reflecting the notion that the researcher is doing less direct interviewing than would otherwise be done in an individual interview. However, a cool detached presence can make the research participants feel like subjects in an experiment and hinder relationship-building between the researcher and the group members. The moderator role is more effective if the researcher genuinely demonstrates high interest coupled with incomplete understanding, reflected in verbal and gestural invitations for participation by group members, and probes for clarification and elaboration.

We would like to offer a few other tips for the researcher conducting a group interview. As in other interviewing situations, it is imperative that the researcher know what he or she wants to find out; the interview guide should function as more of a reference than a script. Very early in the interview, it is useful to ask a question to which everyone can easily respond, and which provides some useful information to the others about each person, such as 'I'd like to start out by asking each of you to share a little about where you live and work. We don't have to go in any order. Bill, will you start?' The cue provided by the researcher, 'We don't have to go in any order' minimizes the likelihood of a round-robin, turn-taking routine, which undermines the conversational quality desired in a group interview. It is fair to say that for most people, the longer they remain silent in a new group, the harder it will be for them to contribute later. It is the interviewer's job to minimize this situation, and foster a positive climate that encourages involvement. In the group interview, the researcher presides over what she or he hopes will be a spontaneous, interesting, and involving discussion around the focus of the study.

Research exercise #13: Planning and conducting a group interview

In planning and conducting a group interview, you will be building on many of the skills and processes you have practiced in previous research exercises.
    You will need several items to carry out this exercise:

- paper and pen
- audio-cassette tape recorder, batteries, electrical cord, extension cord
- external microphone (if you have one)
- audio-cassette tapes
- a quiet room equipped with several chairs

1   The first step: decide on a focus of inquiry. You may want to use a focus of inquiry developed in an earlier exercise, or formulate a new one for this exercise. Recall that a group interview is especially useful for exploring a topic you do not know much about.
2   The second step: develop an interview guide based on your focus of inquiry. For this exercise you should try to conduct at least a one hour group interview, so you will want to develop questions that can be discussed at some length. Use the information presented throughout this chapter on interviewing to help you develop your interview guide.
3   The third step: develop a sampling plan. What sample is suggested by your focus of inquiry? Who do you need to talk with to gain an understanding of your topic? Within this broad group, what different kinds of characteristics or experiences would influence a person's knowledge, experiences, or perspectives on

the topic you are exploring? What types of people are likely to provide you with the greatest breadth of information on your topic? Develop a profile of each person you would ideally like to have as part of your group interview. These ideal profiles are your guides for selecting people for your group, and are not intended to be prescriptions.

4 Find at least four participants for your group interview, besides yourself. Arrange a time and place for the interview that is convenient for the participants, and which will make audio-recording possible (i.e., Are there electrical outlets? Is the room quiet? Can we work uninterrupted?).

5 Prior to conducting the interview:

(a) memorize your interview guide. Even though you will have your interview guide with you during the interview, the more certain you are of what you want to ask, the more likely it is that you will have 'a group conversation with a purpose'.

(b) get together all the materials and equipment you will need to conduct the interview: audio-cassette recorder, batteries, electrical cord, extension cord (just in case), external microphone (if you have one), at least two blank audio-cassette tapes, pen and paper, your interview guide, and any notes. Be sure all equipment is in good working condition.

(c) call participants the night before the interview to remind them of the time and place of the interview.

6 Conduct the group interview. At the start of the interview: a) state the purpose of the interview; b) tell participants generally why they were asked to be involved; c) share your commitment to confidentiality; and then d) ask for permission to tape record the interview. Turn on the tape recorder and get each participant's permission to be tape recorded on tape. Then begin the interview.

7 Immediately after the interview is completed, write out a summary of what happened. This is a chance to reflect on the process and content of the interview. We recommend preparing a reflective summary without first listening to the tape of the interview. Your fresh recollections are worthwhile.

8 Carefully listen to the tape recording of the group interview to assess your interviewing skills. How would you evaluate your interviewing skills? What did you do well? What do you need to improve upon? In conducting another group interview in the future, what would you do the same? What would you do differently?

9 Finally, listen to the tape recording of the group interview for its substantive content. What have you learned about your focus of inquiry? What are the salient themes to pursue, if you were to continue this qualitative study?

The transcripts from group interviews are prepared in accordance with the guidelines for transcribing individual interviews discussed above. In addition, each group member is given a pseudonym and his or her words are transcribed accordingly. It is sometimes a painstaking process to identify who is talking at particular time; immediate transcribing facilitates this effort. Once completed, the group interview transcript is photocopied for use in data analysis.

Documents and Other Sources of Qualitative Data

Finally in this chapter, we want to discuss other sources of data for qualitative research, which may be used as a singular source of data, or combined with observations in the field and in-depth interviews. These other sources of data include such things as personal documents, such as diaries, letters, and autobiographies; public documents, such as organizational memos and policy manuals, written media, literature, and other materials to be found in libraries; and the film media, including photographs, film, and video-tape. We will illustrate the ways in which these different methods of data collection have been used in several recent studies.

Documents

A researcher's focus of inquiry may suggest that the information that will most likely yield an understanding of the phenomenon under study is contained in personal documents. In 1947, psychologist Gordon Allport urged his colleagues to consider personal documents as a critical source of theory-building (Allport, 1947). Allport acknowledged the important work done at the turn of the century by William James, in his exploration of religious experience drawn from the personal confessions of 'great souled persons wrestling with the crisis of their fate' (James, as cited in Allport, 1947: 5). According to Allport, Sigmund Freud was also 'partial to the personal document' (p. 9), a practice that was not well received in the scientific community of his time. Psychology, as well as education and other social science fields, has vacillated on the usefulness and credibility given to data contained in personal documents for illuminating the human experience. The current resurgence of interest in qualitative research and qualitative methods of data collection signal a shift in the intellectual wind.

Several recent studies highlight the usefulness of personal documents in the researcher's search for meaning. For example, to understand more accurately the lives of pioneer women in the early years of the United States, researchers have undertaken the task of searching out the letters and diaries of these women. In painstaking analysis of these personal documents, researchers have uncovered a picture of women's lives much different than our publicly recorded history suggests (see, for example, Myres, 1982; Schlissel, 1982; Smuksta, 1991). Other researchers interested in learning about the lives of living persons have at times been able to gain access to their personal documents, such as diaries or journals. In her study of children's games, Janet Lever (1976) kept diaries of the children's accounts as to how they spent their out of school time and also observed their play. In our own study of the role of television in the lives of college students, we asked seventy-five students to maintain detailed logs of their TV viewing in order to expand what we were learning through in-depth interviews. By combining methods of data collection we also increase the credibility of our findings.

In exploring the lives and experiences of people, individually or as members of organizations, other kinds of documents may be helpful. In examining the lives of college students, campus newspapers, yearbooks, and posters and other notices on public bulletin boards have been studied (Kuh and Andreas, 1991). It is also possible to conduct a qualitative study using only documents, as in a recent study of the popular literature on marriage and retirement (Harbert, Vinick and Ekerdt, 1992). These researchers conducted a qualitative analysis of popular books and articles published between 1960 and 1987 that related to their topic. The themes they identified in the popular media over time indicate changes in the advice given to couples on how to adjust to the husband's retirement, among other things.

Film

In the social science, interest in photographs as research data is a relatively recent experience (Bogdan and Biklen, 1982). One study conducted by these authors involved a comparison of the photographs taken in the 1920s at a state school for students labelled mentally retarded, in which the students looked clean-cut, neat, and well-mannered. This photographic image was in sharp contrast with the way people with intellectual difficulties were portrayed at that time. People with mental handicaps were considered 'society's rogues' and a danger to the welfare of society (Bogdan and Biklen, 1982: 104).

More recently, the use of videotape has found a place among the collection of data collection strategies available to researchers. A research team at Dartmouth College is studying the facial grimaces and symbolic gestures made by politicians during speeches that were videotaped (Berg, 1989). Erickson and Mohatt (1982) videotaped children and teachers in two first grade classrooms over the course of a year to explore the organization of the participation structure in the classroom. There is also a growing body of videotaped study of the interactions between patients and doctors in primary care. Careful analysis has revealed the importance of the context and the continuity of care in the development of satisfactory patient–doctor relationships (Stewart, 1992).

Combining Qualitative Methods of Data Collection

As in all research, the question one poses for study suggests the kind of data that are necessary or potentially useful in trying to answer the question. Many of the qualitative research studies we have referred to throughout this book have pursued multiple methods of data collection to explore the focus of inquiry, combining, for example, in-depth interviews with observations in the natural settings relevant to the study. We provide here another example of combined qualitative methods of data collection. In a comprehensive study of fifty-three women, Valerie Malhotra Bentz explored the process of 'becoming mature', by gathering from these women 'autobiographies from early childhood to the present time, daily diaries, time/memory studies, four separate weekly time schedules, videotaped group discussions, and audiotaped home dinner time discussions with family members and/or friends' (1989: 3). It is noteworthy that Bentz pursued a qualitative investigation after dissatisfaction with the results of a quantitative study of the same women because the 'quantification and systemization of the findings did not capture the essential qualities of the experiences described and discussed by the women' (p. 19).

Preparing a Qualitative Research Proposal: Deciding on Data Collection Methods

In this chapter we have presented a discussion of the main methods of data collection used by qualitative researchers. Which method or methods would be best suited to your focus of inquiry? The student research proposal included in the Appendix illustrates how multiple methods of data collection can be combined in a study. If you have completed the research exercises in this chapter, you have some idea about your level of skill with each of the various methods. Which data collection skills would you like to develop or fine-tune by using them in your own study? All of us get better at being a human instrument by actually carrying out our own research!

Notes

1   We are aware that some qualitative researchers believe that structured interviews are to be avoided in qualitative research (Measor, 1985; Stenhouse, 1984). The range of work cited in this section by qualitative researchers

reflects considerable disagreement with this position. See also, *A Note on structure*, which ends our discussion of interview formats.

2   Many different terms have been used to characterize the amount of structure in an interview. We have chosen the terms *unstructured interview*, *interview guide*, and *interview schedule* to characterize the amount of structure in an interview.

3   This research project was conducted as part of a larger university course on school reform. Teachers at the middle school discovered the value of asking a single broad question through a process designed by the university faculty who are qualitative researchers.

4   The term *focus group* was first used by sociologists (Merton, Fiske and Kendall, 1956). Market researchers have used the term to refer to group interviews that are intended to examine people's preferences for particular products, services, advertisements, even movie endings (Morgan, 1988). These market research *focus groups* follow quite specific criteria for group composition and procedure, and to avoid confusion we will use the term *group interview* here.

References

Allport, G.W. (1947) *The Use of Personal Documents in Psychological Science*, New York: Social Science Research Council.

Anderson, T., Maykut, P.S., Bergdahl, D., Brigson, B., Braun, A., Doherty, D., Effland, B., Haines, J., Hogan, S., Kingsland, D., Peterson, M., Ploor, W. and Windner, M. (1991) 'Academic success at Viterbo: Exploring the experiences and perspectives of high-achieving students', paper presented at the Annual Spring Psychology Symposium, Viterbo College, LaCrosse, Wisconsin.

Becker, H.S. (1970) *Sociological Work: Method and Substance*, Chicago, IL: Aldine.

Belenky, M.F., Clinchy, B.M., Goldberger, N.R. and Tarule, J.M. (1986) *Women's Ways of Knowing: The Development of Self, Voice and Mind*, New York: Basic Books.

Bennett, L. and McAvity, K. (1985) 'Family research: A case for interviewing couples', in Handel, G. (Ed) *The Psychosocial Interior of the Family*, New York: Aldine, pp. 75–94.

Bentz, V.M. (1989) *Becoming Mature: Childhood Ghosts and Spirits in Adult Life*, New York: Aldine de Gruyter.

Berg, B.L. (1989) *Qualitative Research Methods for the Social Sciences*, Boston, MA: Allyn and Bacon.

Boas, F. (1911) *Handbook of American Indian Languages*, Washington, DC: Bureau of American Ethnology, Bulletin 40.

Bogdan, R. and Biklen, S.K. (1982) *Qualitative Research for Education*, Boston, MA: Allyn and Bacon.

BOGDAN, R. and TAYLOR, S. (1975) *Introduction to Qualitative Research Methods: A Phenomenological Approach to the Social Sciences*, New York: Wiley.

BRONFENBRENNER, U. (1979) *The Ecology of Human Development: Experiments by Nature and Design*, Cambridge, MA: Harvard University Press.

BROWN, L.M. and GILLIGAN, C. (1992) *Meeting at the Crossroads: Women's Psychology and Girls' Development*, Cambridge, MA: Harvard University Press.

COLES, R. (1989) *The Call of Stories: Teaching and Moral Imagination*, Boston, MA: Houghton Mifflin.

DALY, K. (1992) 'Parenthood as problematic: Insider interviews with couples seeking adoption', in GILGUN, J.F., DALY, K. and HANDEL, G. (Eds) *Qualitative Methods in Family Research*, Newbury Park, CA: Sage, pp. 103–25.

DENZIN, N.K. (1978) *The Research Act: A Theoretical Introduction to Sociological Methods*, New York: McGraw-Hill.

DEXTER, L.A. (1970) *Elite and Specialized Inteviewing*, Evanston, IL: Northwestern University Press.

ERICKSON, F. and MOHATT, G. (1982) 'Cultural organization of participation structures in two classrooms of Indian students', in SPINDLER, G. (Ed) *Doing the Ethnography of Schooling*, Prospect Heights, IL: Waveland Press, pp. 132–74.

FARRELL, E., PEGUERO, G., LINDSEY, R. and WHITE, R. (1988) 'Giving voice to high school students: Pressure and boredom, ya know what I'm sayin?' *American Educational Research Journal*, **25**, 4, pp. 489–502.

GILGUN, J.F., DALY, K. and HANDEL, G. (Eds) (1992) *Qualitative Methods in Family Research*, Newbury Park, CA: Sage.

GILLIGAN, C. (1982) *In a Different Voice: Psychological Theory and Women's Development*, Cambridge, MA: Harvard University Press.

GLASER, B.G. and STRAUSS, A.L. (1967) *The Discovery of Grounded Theory*, Chicago, IL: Aldine.

HANCOCK, E. (1989) *The Girl Within*, New York: Fawcett Columbine.

HARBERT, E.M., VINICK, B.H. and EKERDT, D.J. (1992) 'Analyzing popular literature: Emergent themes on marriage and retirement', in GILGUN, J.F., DALY, K. and HANDEL, G. (Eds) *Qualitative Methods in Family Research*, Newbury Park, CA: Sage, pp. 263–78.

HOLT, J. (1964) *How Children Fail*, New York: Putman.

HOLT, J. (1967) *How Children Learn*, New York: Putman.

KOZOL, J. (1986) *Death at an Early Age*, New York: Plume.

KRUEGER, R.A. (1988) *Focus Groups: A Practical Guide for Applied Research*, Newbury Park, CA: Sage.

KUH, G.D. and ANDREAS, R.E. (1991) 'It's about time: Using qualitative research methods in student life studies', *Journal of College Student Development*, **32**, pp. 397–405.

LEVER, J. (1976) 'Sex differences in games children play', *Social Problems*, **23**, pp. 478–87.

LINCOLN, Y.S. and GUBA, E.G. (1985) *Naturalistic Inquiry*, Beverly Hills, CA: Sage.

MAGOLDA, M.B. (1992) *Knowing and Reasoning in College: Gender-Related Patterns in Students' Intellectual Development*, San Francisco, CA: Jossey-Bass.

MALINOWSKI, B. (1932) *Argonauts of the Western Pacific*, London: Routledge.

MAYKUT, P.S., BALTZ, A.M., BONDOW, K., BRAGUE, T., CLARK, R., HARRISON, A., JUNE, J., MCDONAH, J., MARTINE, A., PREMO, M., SCHNEIDER, L. and SERVAIS, J. (1992) 'Reflections of older adults: Interim report of research findings', Unpublished manuscript.

MAYKUT, P. and ERICKSON, C. (1991) Involving teachers in carrying out their own qualitative research, Unpublished course materials.

MEAD, M. (1960) *Coming of Age in Somao: A Psychological Study of Primitive Youth for Western Civilization*, New York: Mentor. (Original work published 1928).

MEASOR, L. (1985) 'Interviewing: A strategy in qualitative research', in BURGESS, R.G. (Ed) *Strategies of Educational Research: Qualitative Methods*, Lewes: Falmer Press.

MERTON, R.K., FISKE, M. and KENDALL, P.L. (1956) *The Focused Interview: A Manual of Problems and Procedures*, Glencoe, IL: Free Press.

MISHLER, E.G. (1986) *Research Interviewing: Context and Narrative*, Cambridge, MA: Harvard University Press.

MORGAN, D.L. (1988) *Focus Groups as Qualitative Research*, Newbury Park, CA: Sage.

MYRES, S.L. (1982) *Western Women and the Frontier Experience 1800–1915*, Albuquerque, NM: Univeristy of New Mexico Press.

PATTON, M.Q. (1990) *Qualitative Evaluation and Research Methods* (2nd ed.), Beverly Hills, CA: Sage.

PAYNE, S.L. (1951) *The Art of Asking Questions*, Princeton, NJ: Princeton University Press.

PERRY, W.G. (1970) *Forms of Intellectual and Ethical Development in the College Years: A Scheme*, New York: Holt, Rinehart, and Winston.

PIAGET, J. (1926) *The Language and Thought of Children*, New York: Harcourt, Brace, World.

RICO, C.L. (1983) *Writing the Natural Way: Using Right-brain Techniques to Release your Expressive Powers*, Los Angeles, CA: J.P. Tarcher.

SCHAFER, R., MCCLURG, K., MOREHOUSE, R.M. and MAYKUT, P.S. (1991) 'Exploring the experience of coming home from Desert Storm', Unpublished research materials.

SCHLISSEL, L. (1982) *Women's Diaries of the Westward Journey*, New York: Schocken Books.

SHILS, E.A. (1959) 'Social inquiry and the autonomy of the individual', in LERNER, D. (Ed) *The Human Meaning of the Social Sciences*, Cleveland, OH: Meridian.

SIBBET, D. (1981) *Workbook/guide to Group Graphics*, San Francisco, CA: Graphic Guides, Inc.

SMUKSTA, M. (1991) Work and family: Farm women in Illinois, 1820–1915,

Unpublished doctoral dissertation, Northern Illinois University, Dekalb, Illinois.

STENHOUSE, L. (1984) 'Library access, library use and user education in academic sixth forms: An autobiographical account', in BURGESS, R.G. (Ed) *The Research Process in Educational Settings: Ten Case Studies*, Lewes: Falmer Press.

STEWART, M. (1992) 'Approaches to audiotape and videotape analysis: Interpreting the interactions between patients and physicians', in CRABTREE, B.F. and MILLER, W.L. (Eds) *Doing Qualitative Research*, Newbury Park, CA: Sage.

STODDART, K. (1986) 'The presentation of everyday life', *Urban Life*, **15**, 1, pp. 103–21.

TAYLOR, S.T. and BOGDAN, R. (1984) *Introduction to Qualitative Research Methods: The Search for Meanings* (2nd ed.), New York: Wiley.

WHITBOURNE, S.K. (1986) *The Me I Know: A Study of Adult Identity*, New York: Springer-Verlag.

Part III

Data Analysis

Chapter 8

Qualitative Data Analysis: An Overview

Throughout this book we have cited the work of qualitative researchers who share a common goal: to understand more about a phenomenon of interest. Among them, William Perry (1970) wanted to understand how men's thinking changes as they experience a high quality college education. Mary Belenky and her associates set out to explore how women experience their own learning and describe their ways of knowing (Belenky, Clinchy, Goldberger and Tarule, 1986). Edwin Farrell and his young collaborators wanted to understand more about the lives of students who were at-risk for dropping out of high school (Farrell, Peguero, Lindsey and White, 1988). Lyn Mikel Brown and Carol Gilligan (1992) embarked on a five year 'journey of discovery' by listening to what girls had to say about their thoughts and feelings about themselves and their relationships with others as they grew to adolescence.

Did these qualitative researchers have hunches about what they might discover? Certainly. These researchers are among the experts in their disciplines, and they bring to the research enterprise long histories of education and experience. But in carrying out their qualitative research studies, their hunches were not embodied in hypotheses that they sought to confirm or disconfirm. This distinction in research practice is critical and leads to a substantially different approach to analyzing one's data and arriving at one's findings. The process of qualitative data analysis takes many forms, but it is fundamentally a nonmathematical analytical procedure that involves examining the meaning of people's words and actions. Qualitative research findings are inductively derived from this data.

Each of the researchers described above were seeking understanding of the phenomenon they studied, but each used a somewhat different approach to analyzing their data. Their approaches varied in the level of interpretation they applied to the data and in the actual hands-on procedures they used to conduct their analysis. In an effort to characterize these differences, the well-known qualitative researcher

Anselm Strauss and his colleague Juliet Corbin (1990) describe three approaches to analyzing qualitative data that are instructive for researchers and readers of qualitative research. These three approaches to analysis can be thought of as varying along a continuum ranging from a low level of interpretation and abstraction engaged in by the researcher, to a high level of interpretation and abstraction required for theory building. The first approach, which they compare to the work of a journalist, is that taken by the researcher who intends to present the data without any analysis. The goal is to let the research participants speak for themselves as much as possible, to tell their stories without interpretation. A collection of personal journal entries or autobiographical stories, organized for a coherent reading but not systematically analyzed, would be examples of such an approach (see, for example, Culley, 1985).

The second approach to data analysis Strauss and Corbin identify is that of the researcher who is primarily concerned with accurately describing what she or he has understood, reconstructing the data into a 'recognizable reality' for the people who have participated in the study. This second approach requires some selection and interpretation of the data, and the skilled researcher using this approach becomes adept at 'weaving descriptions, speaker's words, fieldnote quotations, and their own interpretations into a rich and believable descriptive narrative' (1990: 22). Most of the studies described at the beginning of this chapter fit most closely with this descriptive approach to data analysis, although it is sometimes difficult to tell this from their published reports. In more recent discussions of their research, Belenky (1992) and her colleagues have referred to their research approach as 'interpretive-descriptive'. Although description is the primary aim of this second approach to the data, some of the interpretations found in descriptive research suggest an interest in theory building, the third approach to data analysis identified by Strauss and Corbin (1990).

Anselm Strauss draws upon a long history of building theory in the discussion of this third approach to data analysis. Bernard Glaser and Strauss (1967) developed the notion of grounded theory, or theory that is 'inductively derived from the study of the phenomenon it represents' (Strauss and Corbin, 1990: 23). This third approach to data analysis, the development of theory, requires the highest level of interpretation and abstraction from the data in order to arrive at the organizing concepts and tenets of a theory to explain the phenomenon of interest (see, for example, Hancock, 1989; Levinson, 1978).

Our approach to data analysis is Strauss and Corbin's second approach: description, recognizing that some interpretation is necessarily involved in the data analysis process and in selecting the research outcomes that eventually will be reported. We think the term 'interpretative-descriptive' research, used by Belenky accurately characterizes what we do as qualitative researchers and the procedures for data analysis we will describe in the next chapter.

The Qualitative Researcher's Perspective

In qualitative studies, data analysis is best conducted as an early and ongoing research activity. This concomitant action on the part of the researcher allows the research design to emerge over time, suggesting the direction for subsequent data collection efforts. Prior to beginning analysis, however, we want to be especially tuned-in to the human instrument: ourselves. Patton (1990) and others suggest a process called *Epoche* as an initial step in data analysis (Ihde, 1977; Katz, 1987; Moustakas, 1990). According to Katz,

> *Epoche* is a process that the researcher engages in to remove, or at least become aware of prejudices, viewpoints, or assumptions regarding the phenomenon under investigation. *Epoche* helps enable the researcher to investigate the phenomenon from a fresh and open view without prejudgment or imposing meaning too soon. This suspension in judgement is critical in phenomenological investigation and requires the setting aside of the researcher's personal viewpoint in order to see the experience for itself.
>
> (Katz 1987: 36–7)

Thus the qualitative researcher's perspective is perhaps a paradoxical one: it is to be acutely tuned-in to the experiences and meaning systems of others — to indwell — and at the same time to be aware of how one's own biases and preconceptions may be influencing what one is trying to understand.

What can a qualitative researcher understand that cannot be discovered by people looking in on their own settings, examining their own conversations, or exploring their own diaries? What can the astute researcher understand about these insiders that they cannot see for themselves? Rosalie Wax provides an answer to these questions:

> Obtaining something of the understanding of an insider is, for most researchers, only a first step. They expect, in time, to

become capable of thinking and acting within the perspective of two quite different groups, the one in which they were reared and — to some degree — the one they are studying. They will also, at times, be able to *assume a mental position peripheral to both*, a position from which they will be able to perceive and, hopefully, describe the relationships, systems, and patterns of which an inextricably involved insider is not likely to be consciously aware. For what the social scientist realizes is that while the outsider simply does not know the meanings or the patterns, the insider is so immersed that he may be oblivious to the fact that patterns exist at all [italics added].

(Wax, 1991: 3)

The perspective that the skilled researcher brings to data collection and data analysis described by Wax should be instructive to critics who are quick to describe qualitative research as highly subjective. In fact, Lincoln and Guba (1985) argue that the objective–subjective dichotomy used to differentiate research approaches is more aptly viewed as *perspectival*. Insiders, outsiders and researchers each bring a perspective to that which is being studied. What distinguishes the qualitative researcher from the others is disciplined analysis, the topic of the next chapter. We complete this section with a chapter on how to go about communicating the outcomes of a qualitative research study.

References

BELENKY, M.F. (1992, October) 'Bringing balance to the classroom or workplace' paper presented at the Wisconsin Women's Studies Conference, Preconference Workshop, Green Bay, WI.

BELENKY, M.F., CLINCHY, B.M., GOLDBERGER, N.R. and TARULE, J.M. (1986) *Women's Ways of Knowing: The Development of Self, Voice and Mind*, New York: Basic Books.

BROWN, L.M. and GILLIGAN, C. (1992) *Meeting at the Crossroads: Women's Psychology and Girls' Development*, Cambridge, MA: Harvard University Press.

CULLEY, M. (Ed) (1985) *A Day at a Time: The Diary Literature of American Women from 1764 to the Present*, New York: The Feminist Press at the City University of New York.

FARRELL, E., PEGUERO, G., LINDSEY, R. and WHITE, R. (1988) 'Giving voice to high school students: Pressure, boredom, "ya know what I'm sayin?" ', *American Educational Research Journal*, **25**, pp. 489–502.

GLASER, B.G. and STRAUSS, A.L. (1967) *The Discovery of Grounded Theory*, Chicago, IL: Aldine.

HANCOCK, E. (1989) *The Girl Within*, New York: Fawcett Columbine.

IHDE, D. (1977) *Experimental Phenomenology*, New York: G.P. Putnam.

KATZ, L. (1987) '*The Experience of Personal Change*', unpublished doctoral dissertation, Union Graduate School, Union Institute, Cincinnati, OH.

LEVINSON, D.J. (1978) *The Seasons of a Man's Life*, New York: Ballantine.

LINCOLN, Y.S. and GUBA, E.G. (1985) *Naturalistic Inquiry*, Beverly Hills, CA: Sage.

MOUSTAKAS, C. (1990) *Heuristic Research: Design, Methodology, and Applications*, Newbury Park, CA: Sage.

PATTON, M.Q. (1990) *Qualitative Evaluation and Research Methods* (2nd ed.), Beverly Hills, CA: Sage.

PERRY, W.G. (1970) *Forms of Intellectual and Ethical Development in the College Years: A Scheme*, New York: Holt, Rinehart, and Winston.

STRAUSS, A. and CORBIN, J. (1990) *Basics of Qualitative Research: Grounded Theory Procedure and Techniques*, Newbury Park, CA: Sage.

WAX, R.H. (1971) *Doing Fieldwork: Warning and Advice*, Chicago, IL: University of Chicago Press.

Chapter 9

Qualitative Data Analysis: Using the Constant Comparative Method

Our approach to data analysis is to understand more about the phenomenon we are investigating and to describe what we learn with a minimum of interpretation. We are interested in developing *propositions*: statements of fact inductively derived from a rigorous and systematic analysis of the data. In arriving at these propositions, we want to stay close to the research participants' feelings, thoughts and actions as they broadly relate to our focus of inquiry. There are several seasoned qualitative researchers whose work is the basis of our own. We have found Glaser and Strauss's (1967) *constant comparative method* of data analysis well-suited to our purposes, although this method of analysis was developed for theory building. Lincoln and Guba (1985) have added important procedural detail to the steps involved in analyzing data using the constant comparative method that have proven essential to rigorous analysis, particularly when one is working with a research team. Our analytic procedures also draw on the work of Steven Taylor and Robert Bogdan (1984), and we have incorporated several of David Sibbet's (1981) group graphics concepts and procedures in refining our methodology. Many of our students have contributed in important ways to the procedures outlined here.

An Inductive Approach to Data Analysis

One of the defining characteristics of qualitative research is an inductive approach to data analysis. As Goertz and LeCompte (1981) note, a deductive approach to data analysis is characteristic of the traditional scientific method; hypotheses are generated prior to beginning the study, indicating the relevant data to be collected (the variables); the resulting data is mathematically analyzed to determine whether the hypotheses have been confirmed or disconfirmed. Inductive approaches to data analysis take quite a different path. Data are collected that relate to a focus of inquiry. Hypotheses are not generated a priori and thus the relevant variables for data collection are not predetermined. The data are not grouped according to predetermined categories. Rather, what becomes important to analyze emerges from the data itself, out of a process of inductive reasoning.

The constant comparative method is one way to conduct an inductive analysis of qualitative data (Glaser and Strauss, 1967; Lincoln and Guba, 1985). We have found that this method provides the beginning researcher with a clear path for engaging in analysis of substantial amounts of data in a way that is both challenging and illuminating. We will describe the constant comparative method in greater detail after discussing procedures for preparing the raw data from the field for analysis. Alternative methods of qualitative data analysis can be found in various books on the topic (see, for example, Bogdan and Biklen, 1982; Miles and Huberman, 1984; Patton, 1990).

Preparing the Data for Analysis

The challenging task of making sense out of a quickly accumulating pile of field notes, audio-tapes, and documents is facilitated by the quick and efficient transfer of this raw data into clearly readable form for data analysis. All field notes should be typed. Audio-taped interviews must be transcribed. Documents that are handwritten and unclear should also be typed, if possible.

Coding data pages to their sources

Data analysis is best conducted using photocopies of all data. However, prior to photocopying, it is helpful to code each page of data. Data pages come from one or more sources, such as interview transcripts, field notes or documents, and it is important to maintain an easy way of identifying these various sources in the growing mound of data you will amass. There are clearly various ways one can code data pages to their sources; we review one strategy here. In the upper right-hand corner of each page of data, include a code for the type of data, the source of the data, and the page number of the particular data set, such as pages of a transcript. For example, the fifth page (5) of a transcript (T) from an interview with Marie (M) is coded in the top right-hand corner of the page as T/M-5. The coding for the first page (1) of field notes from observing (O) at Granger Elementary Schools is coded O/ GES-1. As data collection efforts become increasingly complex, more elaborate codes can be developed. Once all the data pages have been coded to their source, photocopying can proceed.

The photocopies of the data pages will eventually be divided into 'chunks of meaning' (Marshall, 1981) for analysis, and each chunk or unit of meaning will need to be coded to its source. Careful attention to recording the source of all data pages early in the data collection and analysis process will allow you to return to the original data set when necessary, to study the units of data in their fuller context.

Unitizing the data

Once all data have been photocopied, the next step is to identify the chunks or units of meaning in the data, a process referred to by Lincoln and Guba (1985) as *unitizing* the data. At this point we strongly recommend setting aside the original data set and using the photocopies for unitizing and subsequent data analysis. In order to carry out the unitizing process, you will need the photocopies of the data, several packages of blank 5″ × 8″ index cards, scissors, tape, and a pen.[1]

The process of qualitative data analysis is one of culling for meaning from the words and actions of the participants in the study, framed by the researcher's focus of inquiry. This search for meaning is accomplished by first identifying the smaller units of meaning in the data, which will later serve as the basis for defining larger categories of meaning. In order to be useful for analysis, each unit of meaning identified in the data must stand by itself, i.e., it must be understandable without additional information, except for knowledge of the researcher's focus of inquiry (Lincoln and Guba, 1985). Note, however, that units of meaning in an interview transcript may be in response to a question that needs to be included with the unit of meaning to make sense.

We will use examples from our study of the lives and perspectives of people who grew up in the 1920s and 1930s to illustrate the concept of unitizing (Maykut, *et al.*, 1992). The older adults in our sample participated in in-depth interviews. One of the questions they were asked was 'How do people gain wisdom?' One interviewee's short response formed a single unit of meaning:

Interviewer: In your opinion, how do people gain wisdom?
Interviewee: Thinkin'. You can get more by thinkin' than by any other way.
Interviewer: Thinking about what?
Interviewee: Think clearly.

A unit of meaning may be a full paragraph:

Interviewer: How do people gain wisdom?
Interviewee: Through reading and studying and experiences, and . . . between my husband and I, we were always frank about all conditions. And I did my part, which was keeping house and teaching school. And he did his part, which was earning a living. We respected each other . . . and I didn't interfere with what he had to do, and he didn't interfere with what I had to do. Since I've been on my own, I know I have gained a lot more insight in the financial things than I had before, because that was his thing. So, I have kept on learning, and am still learning, and I think I have successfully weathered the storm of finances, too. I haven't gone backwards since I've been on my own. I've been able to go forward.

It is likely that some units of meaning will be quite a bit longer than a paragraph, especially in studies where participants are telling life stories.

Units of meaning are identified by carefully reading through transcripts, field notes and documents. In the procedure we use for data analysis, these units will eventually be cut from the photocopies of the data for easy manipulation. But prior to cutting, you can do the necessary unitizing of the data. Carefully read through the transcript copy (or other data source). When you identify a unit of meaning, draw a line across the page to separate this unit of meaning from the next unit. Then indicate in the left margin where the unit is located in the data set. For example, T/N-12 refers to the 12th page of the transcript from an interview with Nancy. The next step is to indicate in a word or phrase the essence of the unit's meaning. Print this word or phrase beneath your notation of the data source.

Using this procedure for unitizing, you will easily be able to go back to the intact transcript, field notes or other data source to read the excerpt in its fuller context, should further clarification of meaning be needed. For beginning researchers we recommend that every piece of one's transcripts, field notes, and documents be unitized; no stray pieces should remain after you complete this process.

The next step in unitizing is to cut apart the units of meaning that you have identified in the data, and to tape each unit onto separate 5″ × 8″ index cards. (In the discussion of data analysis that follows, we

Figure 9.1: Unitizing the data

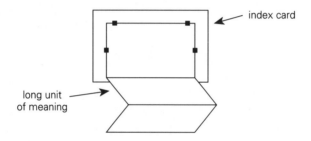

```
                        T/N-12              │                          T/N-13

  T/N-12    ~~~~~~~~~~~                │  T/N-13    ~~~~~~~~~~~
  gaining   ~~~~~~~~~~~                │  view of   ~~~~~~~~~~~
  wisdom    ~~~~~~~~~~~                │  death     ~~~~~~~~~~~
            ~~~~~~~~~~~                │
            ~~~~~~~~~~~                │────────────────────────
                                              T/N-13    ~~~~~~~~~~~
  T/N-12    ~~~~~~~~~~~                │  WWII      ~~~~~~~~~~~
  pearl of  ~~~~~~~~~~~                │  experience ~~~~~~~~~~~
  wisdom    ~~~~~~~~~~~                │            ~~~~~~~~~~~
            ~~~~~~~~~~~                │            ~~~~~~~~~~~
                                      │            ~~~~~~~~~~~
```

Figure 9.2: Unitizing a long unit of meaning

index card

long unit
of meaning

will primarily use the example of interview data to illustrate the process, although it applies to most forms of qualitative data.) Recall that some units of meaning may be as short as a sentence; others may be quite long, but it is still possible to use the index card system by taping the top of the unit onto the card and folding up the remaining part of the page.

Lincoln and Guba (1985) recommend that researchers label each data card on the blank side with additional information that may prove important as the analysis proceeds, such as the occupation, gender, or age of interviewees, or the site of a particular observation or interaction, such as, in the hallway outside the classroom. For example, we have recently been engaged in a study of young adults' experience of opposite-sex friendships, in which pairs of current friends participated in a joint interview (Maykut *et al.*, 1992). In unitizing the data from these interviews, we have indicated the gender of each friend in the dyad who is speaking on the back of each data card. We know from recent qualitative and quantitative research that there appear to be gender differences in the experience of cross-sex friendships. We wanted information on gender easily available to us on the back of the cards, but not so obviously noted that it might influence our data analysis.

Physical arrangements for data analysis

In conducting scientific experiments, researchers often need a laboratory. In conducting qualitative research, the laboratory for data collection is in the natural settings where social phenomenon occur. The qualitative researcher does, however, benefit from having a physical space for carrying out data analysis. The procedures we discuss in this chapter rely on the availability of a room with walls on which visual displays of data and other information can be adhered to with tape, tacks, pins, etc. You will also need several large pieces of paper; especially handy are end rolls of paper sometimes available from newspapers or print shops. A supply of blank index cards, tape, and markers are also necessary. While there are other ways to go about the process of data analysis, we have found the visual 'wallpaper' approach highly workable, and absolutely essential if one is working with a research team.

Working with a Research Team

We pause in this discussion of the data analysis process to talk briefly about working with a team, a feature that becomes especially useful in qualitative data analysis. Certainly interests, resources and time make it difficult to design and implement a research project with others. However, our own experience testifies to the tremendous potential benefits of working with at least one other researcher with whom you share an interest. The dynamic of the fine-tuned research team can boost energy, foster insight and add to the credibility of the study. In addition, the checks and balances inherent in team-based data analysis increases the trustworthiness of the analysis (Lincoln and Guba, 1985).

If you are able to work with a research team, prior to engaging in further data analysis, we recommend gathering together as a team to generate some ground rules for working together. These rules or reminders are designed to help the researchers work together productively and cooperatively. Most people have had experiences working in groups and have gained some clear ideas about what facilitates the group process. As the team carries out its work together, and new rules become needed, the list of ground rules can be expanded. In our work with colleagues and students, a few ground rules show up with some frequency:

- Come to each team meeting on time.
- Come to each team meeting prepared.
- Bring snacks.
- Don't agree for the sake of agreeing, no matter how late in the day it gets.
- Don't make it personal — 'I like you, but I don't agree with you.'
- Keep in mind: ALL OF US KNOW MORE THAN ONE OF US.

Post the team's ground rules in the room where your team works and refer to them when necessary.

In our continuing discussion of data analysis, we will describe procedures for the researcher working alone and, where appropriate, point out how research team members can collaborate in the process.

Discovery

At the beginning of Chapter 5 we introduced the practice of using a researcher's journal. When you wrote down recurring ideas, questions, thoughts, ect., in your journal, you were engaging in an important first step in qualitative data analysis: *discovery* (Taylor and Bogdan, 1984). The goal of this initial step is to identify a large array of potentially important experiences, ideas, concepts, themes, etc., in the data. Discovery occurs throughout data collection, as recurring ideas are recorded in one's journal, and begins the formal process of data analysis.

We have found the accordion to be a useful metaphor in thinking about the somewhat complicated process of qualitative data analysis. The word accordion is derived from German and French words meaning agreement and harmony. The accordion is a portable musical instrument with a small keyboard and free metal rods, that sound when air is forced passed by them by pleated bellows operated by the musician. The action of playing an accordion is one of pulling these bellows apart with both hands, while pressing the appropriate keys, and then squeezing the bellows together to create the harmonic sound. In qualitative data analysis, the discovery step metaphorically pulls apart the bellows just a bit, widening the array of potentially salient aspects of the phenomenon under study.

The discovery process is a beginning search for the important meanings in what people have said to you in interviews or what you have observed in the field, in documents, etc. To begin analyzing the

Figure 9.3:   Illustration of data analysis process

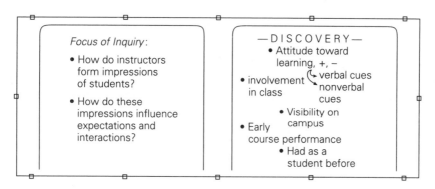

data, you first carefully reread the data you have collected so far, and the notes in your journal, becoming very familiar with these data and ideas. Then ask yourself the following questions: What are the recurring words, phrases, and topics in the data? What are the concepts that the interviewees use to capture what they say or do, (such as 'spacing out', 'hanging out', 'just putting in time', 'on the go')? Can you think of other concepts that capture some recurring phenomenon in the data, that help sensitize you to recognize it when it occurs again (Blumer, 1969)? Can you identify any emerging themes in your data, expressed as a phrase, proposition or question? Do you see any patterns?

On a large clean sheet of paper begin to answer these questions. Generate an array of recurring concepts, phrases, topics, patterns and themes grounded in (drawn from) your interviews, field notes, documents or other sources of data. Write all over the paper; you need not constrain your thinking by a linear listing of items. You do not, however, need to do an exhaustive listing: This is a beginning effort at stating what is in the data. Post your discovery sheet in the room you have set aside for data analysis. If you are working with a research team, generate the list together and post it so all team members can see it. Also write out your focus of inquiry on large paper and tape it up next to your discovery sheet.

In order to illustrate the process of data analysis, we will use a small study we conducted exploring how college instructors form impressions of students (Maykut *et al.*, 1991). You can see in the illustration above our focus of inquiry and discovery sheet.

The discovery step is a first step at uncovering what is salient in one's data. We want to emphasize that the information generated on this first large sheet of paper is *not* something to hold onto as the final outcomes of the study. It is just a start.

The Constant Comparative Method

The *constant comparative method* of analyzing qualitative data combines inductive category coding with a simultaneous comparison of all units of meaning obtained (Glaser and Strauss, 1967). As each new unit of meaning is selected for analysis, it is compared to all other units of meaning and subsequently grouped (categorized and coded) with similar units of meaning. If there are no similar units of meaning, a new category is formed. In this process there is room for continuous refinement; initial categories are changed, merged, or omitted; new categories are generated; and new relationships can be discovered (Goertz and LeCompte, 1981).

Lincoln and Guba provide us with a useful description of the categorizing and coding process:

> The essential tasks of categorizing are to bring together into provisional categories those cards [data cards] that apparently relate to the same content; to devise rules that describe category properties and that can, ultimately, be used to justify the inclusion of each card that remains to be assigned to the category as well as to provide a basis for later tests of replicability; and to render the category internally consistent.
>
> (Lincoln and Guba, 1985: 347)

In the categorizing and coding process the researcher seeks to develop a set of categories that provide 'a "reasonable" reconstruction of the data' she or he has collected (1985: 347). Our procedure for categorizing data presented in this section is based primarily on the description of the constant comparative method provided by Lincoln and Guba, with some adaptions of our own.

The constant comparative method of data analysis can be illustrated as shown in Figure 9.4.

We will describe each of these steps in detail, using the exploration of how college instructors form impressions of students as our example. If you are working with a research team, please read 'you' to mean 'all of the team members'.

Inductive category coding

To begin this process, be sure you have all the necessary materials in front of you: unitized index cards, research journal, focus of inquiry

Figure 9.4: Constant comparative method of data analysis

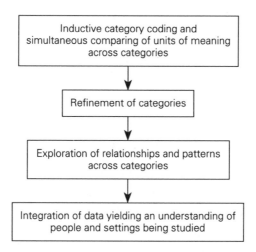

sheet, and your initial discovery sheet of recurring words, concepts, and themes. You will also need markers, tape, several blank 5″ × 8″ index cards, large sheets of paper, and a paper cutter, if you are using end rolls (which we strongly recommend). By this time you should be quite familiar with the data you have collected up to this point. (Recall that data analysis begins early in the study, after some of the data have accumulated, and continues at intervals until the study is completed.)

Next, tape up a large sheet of paper on the wall to be used as your working surface, and also as a record of your analysis. The visual record of your work contributes to the 'audit trail' available to you and others who are interested in tracing the path from your initial ideas to your research outcomes (Lincoln and Guba, 1985). You will have several pieces of large paper filled by the time you finish your analysis.

Review your initial discovery sheet of recurring concepts and themes, and combine any ideas that overlap with one another. Then select one prominent idea from your sheet. Write this idea on an index card and tape it to the left hand side of your large paper. This word/phrase is your first provisional coding category. Each of the words/phrases on your discovery sheet is considered a provisional category. Note, however, that these are provisional categories, derived from your broad familiarity with the data, and some or all of the provisional categories may be eliminated in the final categorization scheme.

Next, carefully look through your unitized data cards to see if you have one or more cards that fit your first provisional category. When you find a card that you think fits the first provisional category, tape the

Figure 9.5: First provisional coding category

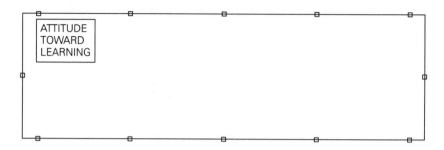

Figure 9.6: Continuing provisional coding categories

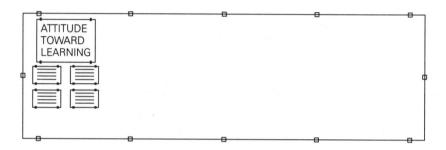

card under the category card. When you find a second data card that you think fits this first category, reread the first data card and compare it to the second card. Decide whether the second card 'looks like' or 'feels like' the meaning of the first data card. If it does, tape it beneath the first data card. Examine your data for other cards that fit this first provisional category, comparing each card to the others already catego-rized to see if they fit together.

If a data card does not fit this first provisional category, you will be categorizing it elsewhere (described below). It is possible that you will have no data cards that fit a provisional category drawn from your discovery sheet — this just means that what you initially thought was a salient idea was not borne out by the data itself.

The 'look/feel-alike' criteria was advanced by Lincoln and Guba (1985) as a way of describing the emergent process of categorizing qualitative data. The researcher asks himself or herself whether the unit of meaning on one card is very similar to the unit of meaning on another card. In this systematic and painstaking way, salient categories of meaning are inductively derived.

If you are working with a team, team members examine their data for units of meaning that potentially fit the first provisional category.

Figure 9.7: *Expanding provisional categories*

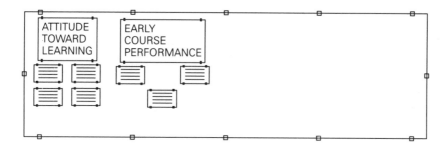

These data cards are read aloud and the team decides whether data cards fit together under the category, based on the the look/feel-alike criteria. This is a time-consuming process but one which substantially increases the credibility of the team's inductive process. If the team decides a data card fits the look/feel-alike criteria, tape it beneath the first provisional category card. Examine the data for other cards that fit this first provisional category.

When you come across a data card that does not fit the first provisional category based on the look/feel-alike criteria, examine your discovery sheet of ideas and see if the contents of the data card fit any of these other provisional categories. If so, write the second provisional category on an index card and place it to the right of the first category. Tape the data card beneath it. Examine your data for other cards that fit this second provisional category, comparing each card to the others already categorized to see if they fit together based on the look/feel-alike criteria.

When you find that a data card does not fit any of the provisional categories printed on the discovery sheet, begin a new category and tentatively name it. You can use a relevant word or phrase, or the first sentence of a quote from the data card as the category name. Tape the data card under this new provisional category. Examine your data for other cards that fit this new provisional category, comparing each card to the others already categorized to see if they fit together based on the look/feel-alike criteria.

Of course, you only have a vague idea of what your categories mean at this point. The process of inductively deriving important meaning from the data requires tolerance for the initial ambiguousness of the look/feel-alike criteria. Try to stay with the look/feel-alike criteria as the basis for deciding whether a data card: a) is a look/feel-alike of the cards that have already been placed in one provisional category; b) is

Figure 9.8: *Adding new categories*

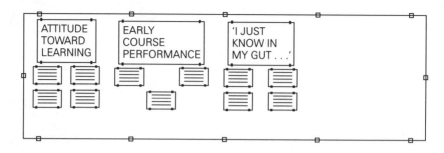

a look/feel-alike of one of the provisional categories still on the discovery sheet', or c) represents a new category. Proceed in this manner until you have accumulated 6–8 cards in a category, at which time you will want to write a *rule for inclusion* for additional data cards (Lincoln and Guba, 1985), a procedure described below.

It is helpful to know that new categories are likely to evolve at a rapid pace early in the analysis process, and it is not unusual to develop thirty or more categories quickly. The accordion metaphor may be helpful here. This expansive process of categorizing data is analogous to fully pulling apart the folds of the accordion, which is necessary for the eventual harmonic synthesis to occur. Like an accordionist, the qualitative researcher methodically pulls apart the meaning contained in the data, enabling her or him to eventually reconstruct the important melodies contained in the phenomenon being studied.

The number of categories derived from any particular data set will depend on the focus of inquiry, the type(s) of data collected and the analytic skills of the researcher. Lincoln and Guba (1985) note that early in analysis new categories quickly emerge, but the rate of new category development is substantially reduced after about fifty categories.

Three additional aspects of the categorizing process deserve attention. First, as your categorization scheme evolves, it may become evident that some data cards fit into more than one category. We suggest copying these data cards and taping them up under the appropriate categories. Second, if you recall information that counts as data for your study, but do not have it in your prepared transcripts, field notes, journal, etc., write out the information on a blank index card so it can be added to the analysis. For instance, you may remember something an interviewee said before the interview was tape recorded that emerges as important in the process of data analysis. You can write this information on a card and tape it up under the relevant category. Third, as you proceed with analysis you may begin to see data cards that are clearly outside the important content of the study. These data cards can be put in a category (or box) labeled 'miscellaneous'. Before the analysis is completed these miscellaneous cards will be reviewed again for possible inclusion (Lincoln and Guba, 1985).

Refinement of Categories

Writing rules of inclusion

When several cards have been grouped together using the look/feel-alike criteria, carefully reread these data cards. What are the properties or characteristics of the group of cards clustered together under the category? Your goal here is to distill the meaning carried in the cards, and write a rule that will serve as the basis for including (or excluding) subsequent data cards in the category. We have found that the process of writing rules for inclusion is facilitated by either jotting down on a separate piece of paper the properties as you identify them, or underlining or highlighting the quotes or other information on each card that led you to its current categorization. Lincoln and Guba (1985) suggest writing the rule for inclusion as a *propositional statement.* As Taylor and Bogdan succinctly state, 'A proposition is a general statement of fact grounded in the data' (1984: 134). In other words, a propositional statement is one that conveys the *meaning* that is contained in the data cards gathered together under a category name. Rules for inclusion, stated as propositions, begin to reveal what you are learning about the phenomenon you are studying and are a critical step in arriving at your research outcomes.

Let us return to our study of how college instructors form impressions of students for an example of rule writing. Our first provisional category was 'Attitude Toward Learning', as illustrated above. The data cards grouped together under this category included quotes from instructors such as 'I notice whether a student pays attention in class, whether they seem interested in what I'm saying', and 'Sleeping in class is something that really insults me, and creates a pretty bad impression.' Our cards also included data indicating that instructors' notice which students come to class prepared, ask 'good' questions, and contribute to discussion. The rule for inclusion we developed, stated as a proposition was: Instructors form impressions of students based on many verbal and nonverbal behaviors of students that say to them, in effect, 'I do (or do not) want to learn.' We decided that our initial category name —

Attitude Toward Learning — was not as descriptive as it could be, and renamed it: 'I Do (or do not) Want to Learn' Behaviors. We prepared a new card, which contained the new category name and a code for it, and the rule for inclusion, stated as a proposition:

Category name and code: 'I Do (or do not) Want to Learn' Behaviors (LB)

Rule for inclusion: Instructors form impressions of students based on many verbal and nonverbal behaviors of students that say to them, in effect, 'I do (or do not) want to learn.'

We want to emphasize that rule writing is more than a restating of the category name. You are not simply stating what kinds of data cards are in the category, but what 'statement of fact' you tentatively propose, based on your data. In our example, recall the focus of inquiry: How do instructors form impressions of students? Our beginning analysis revealed that instructors form impressions based on, in part, verbal and nonverbal behaviors of students that say, in effect, 'I do (or do not) want to learn.' Our rule for inclusion, stated as a proposition, reflected the essential meaning contained in the data cards.

One of the strategies that can be helpful for developing propositional statements is to keep in mind sentence stems that emphasize the meaning contained in the cards: I (We) are finding out that people believe . . . (think, experience, value, identify, etc.). Of course, the sentence depends on who or what you are studying, but the point is that you need to make the shift from categorizing units of meaning, to preparing a statement that reflects the collective meaning contained in the cards within each category. It is often a time-consuming process to get to a propositional statement for one category.

We offer a few more examples of rules for inclusion, stated as propositions. The examples below are from a study of the life and perspectives of people who grew up during the 1920s and 1930s (Maykut *et al.*, 1992):

Category name and code: Prized Possessions (PP)

Rule for inclusion: Prized material possessions are valued because of their connection to other people who either gave them the item or owned it themselves.

Category name: Preparation for Death (PD)

Rule for inclusion:	Individuals feel more prepared for their own death than they do for the deaths of others.

In continuing the process of data analysis, each data card is reread to determine whether it fits the category rule or if it should be categorized elsewhere. As you refine categories, it is likely that you will find data cards that, on closer scrutiny, do not fit their initial category placement; they may fit another category or form the basis of a new category.

Categorizing positive and negative instances

It is likely that in the process of categorizing data cards, you will find both positive and negative instances of a particular phenomenon in the data. For example, in our study of older adults, we found that most of the participants felt more prepared for their own death than they did for the deaths of others (positive instances). However, one of the individuals interviewed did not feel prepared for death — hers or anyone else's (a negative instance). What do you do with these 'negative cases'? While some qualitative researchers insist on revising propositional statements to account for all cases (see Kidder, 1981), most researchers derive propositional statements from a substantial accumulation of positive instances (Taylor and Bogdan, 1984).

Coding data cards to their categories

The refinement of categories requires yet another step. Once the researcher has written a rule for inclusion for a category, he or she must develop a code that can be used to mark the data cards that comprise the category. Category codes for the examples above are indicated by the capital letters in parentheses, accompanying the category name. Codes should reflect the meaning of the category and provide a recognizable cue. The category code is placed on the top of each data card. It is important to know that the coding of data to their categories also substantially increases the mobility of the data set. Data cards can now be collected into similarly coded envelopes, folders, or shoe boxes to be moved to other work spaces. An unfortunate mishap which sends your data sprawling can easily be remedied.

The development of a rule for inclusion shifts the criteria for categorizing remaining data from look/feel-alike to the propositional rule statement. Data cards that fit the rule are taped up under the rule, and those that do not fit are categorized elsewhere (or as miscellaneous). However, the rule-based categories can themselves be modified or even eliminated if in the process of analyzing data the propositional rule statements do not hold, i.e., are no longer true based on an analysis of the remaining data.

To review, a rule for inclusion is developed for a category when several data cards have been clustered under it based on the look/feel-alike criterion. The rule for inclusion is inductively derived from the properties or characteristics of the initial set of data cards clustered together under it. The rule for inclusion is stated as a proposition that summarizes the meaning contained in the data cards. Data cards that on closer examination do not fit the resulting rule are categorized elsewhere. Remaining data are now included in or excluded from a category based on its rule for inclusion, not the look/feel-alike criterion. Data cards are coded to their rule-based categories. Data analysis continues until all data cards have been categorized into a substantive category or the miscellaneous pile.

When all data cards have been categorized, review the categories for any overlap and ambiguity. Are the cards in each category clearly similar? Are the cards in separate categories clearly different? Adjust and redefine categories and rules if necessary. Lastly, review the data cards in the miscellaneous pile to see if they can be meaningfully added to the categorized data.

Research exercise #14: Practicing unitizing, categorizing and writing rules for inclusion

Learning to carry out qualitative data analysis as described in this section takes practice; although we all analyze what we read or hear to some extent, doing it *systematically* is quite a different matter. We provide the following exercise as one means of practicing analysis with a relatively small data set and without the need for transcribing or typing field notes.

You will need the cooperation of several people for this exercise. You can ask people individually to help you out, or obtain access and permission from a pre-formed group, such as a class from a local high school or college or members of a community club. Try to get the participation of a dozen people. You will also need paper and pens for each participant, and the materials for data analysis discussed above: large paper, paper cutter, tape, index cards, markers and a place to work.

1 Ask the people in your sample to write their response to an open-ended question that is of particular interest to you. Here you are essentially asking an essay question for which there really is no right answer! Ideally, you could develop a focus of inquiry and a broad, open-ended interview question that would help you pursue your inquiry. We offer some possible questions for your use that we have found useful for eliciting interesting and different perspectives. Be sure to give the interviewee some time to reflect on the question before writing, since they are not very likely to have been asked any of these questions before.

- How does a person gain wisdom?
- What have you learned how to do by watching television?
- How would you describe yourself today to someone in a letter, if they had never had the chance to meet you in person? Please describe yourself in such a way that you would recognize yourself in the description.
- How would you describe a successful life?
- If you were to read two conflicting news reports, how would you decide which is the truth?
- What has been the most powerful learning experience for you?

2   Ask participants to respond to the question in writing, and request that they write or print clearly. Assure participants that you are the only person who will see their response. You might also want to ask them to omit their names from the paper, particularly if you think that there is the likelihood that they will be more truthful if their responses are anonymous. Depending on your question, you may want to ask participants to indicate at the top of the paper their age, gender, years in school or other information potentially relevant in understanding their responses.

3   The written responses that you obtain from the participants are a kind of document that can be analyzed using the constant comparative method. To prepare the data, follow the directions for unitizing the data described earlier. Be sure to photocopy all documents prior to cutting and taping units of meaning onto index cards.

4   To begin analysis, prepare a discovery sheet, writing down the recurring ideas in the data.

5   Use the constant comparative method to analyze your data, following the procedural steps described in this chapter.

6   You are likely to end up with several propositional statements that together provide an answer to the question you posed to the participants.

Exploration of Relationships and Patterns across Categories

If you have followed the data analysis procedure outlined in this chapter in an actual research project or for *Research exercise #14*, you have in hand several well-written propositional rule statements that are the rules for inclusion for each of your categories. You also have many data cards grouped with each propositional statement. Remember the accordianist who was pulling apart the bellows of her musical instrument, in preparation for the harmonic synthesis? It is time to carefully and systematically squeeze the bellows (the data) together to create a sight and sound somewhat different but accurately reflective of the data with which you started.

The focus for this step in analysis is to closely examine the many propositional statements that have emerged from your careful analysis. Some of your propositions are likely to be more important than others in contributing to an understanding of your focus of inquiry. These propositions are the roughly formed outcomes of your study, but are as yet unconnected to each other in meaningful ways. Some of your propositions will probably stand alone, sufficiently describing some aspect of the phenomenon under study. Other propositions are likely to relate to each other in important ways. Your goal is to study your propositions for those that stand alone and for those that form salient relationships and patterns. We refer to the propositions that stand alone and to the propositions that are formed by connecting two or more other propositions as *outcome propositions.*

In our study of people who grew up in the 1920s and 1930s, there were several connections we could see across the propositional rule statements that resulted from our categorization of the data (Maykut *et al.*, 1992). For example, people's views on their own death were related to their belief in an afterlife, the quality of the life they had lived so far and the options they saw for their own future. These different aspects were first identified separately in the data, as categories; the relationship among them became evident as we studied the propositions and data further. A pattern of differences based on gender was also evident in the data: as girls and boys growing up, the people in our sample were subject to different expectations about how they should spend their time and what they could accomplish in life.

Examining a substantial number of propositions for possible connections is a challenging task, sometimes aided by brief periods of time away from your data. Interested others can provide assistance by hearing about your ideas, asking questions, and perhaps suggesting connections they see in your data. Working in a research team can also be beneficial, as each team member attends to different aspects of the phenomenon and tries out ideas with the team.

Returning to the field

A qualitative approach to inquiry emphasizes an emergent research design process. Data analysis is an early and ongoing research activity, with the results from early data analysis guiding subsequent data collection efforts (see Figure 4.1). But when is data analysis complete? There are theoretical and practical answers to this question. Clearly, it is desirable to end both data collection and data analysis when no new or relevant information is being uncovered, a process that has been described as reaching 'redundancy' in the data (Lincoln and Guba, 1985). Strauss and Corbin recommend that data collection and analysis continue until the 'theoretical saturation point is reached' (1990: 188), and the categories and relationships between categories are well supported. Important unanswered questions direct further data collection efforts.

There are, however, other constraints that can limit the extent of sampling and analysis in a given research project. The academic year ends, resources of time and money run out, and unexpected realities impinge upon one's careful planning. The qualitative researcher is advised to follow the carpenter's rule: estimate the amount of time it will take for the job and then double it. Other recommendations: Sample purposefully, and prepare and analyze data in a timely manner.

Integration of Data and Writing Up the Research

The last step in data analysis is to write about what you have heard, seen and now understand, to create the harmonic sound of data coming together in narrative form to make sense of the phenomenon you have studied. We include this brief paragraph here to acknowledge that writing up one's research is part of the analytic process. Pondering the substance and sequence of the report requires a rethinking of the data, often yielding new insights and understanding. We pursue the topic of writing about the outcomes of qualitative research in the next chapter.

Trustworthiness of the Research

The procedures for data collection and data analysis presented in this book include several elements that increase the trustworthiness of one's research findings. After Guba (1981; Lincoln and Guba, 1985), we apply the concept of trustworthiness in designing and carrying out our own qualitative research and in evaluating the work of other qualitative researchers. The question of trustworthiness essentially asks: To what extent can we place confidence in the outcomes of the study? Do we believe what the researcher has reported?

Perhaps you already know quite a lot about the features of a research study that give you confidence in the reported outcomes. For example, you probably appreciate a research report that provides clear and detailed information about a) the purpose of the study; b) how participants and/or settings became part of the sample; c) the specific people and/or settings studied; d) the data collection and analysis procedures used, and e) the findings or outcomes. Detailed information about purpose and methods lays the research process open for readers, inviting their consideration and scrutiny of the work.

A detailed description of the research process and outcomes provides readers with a basis for judging the credibility of a study. It allows them to look closely at the sample and the specific procedures for data collection and analysis and will contribute to (or lessen) their level of trust in the reported outcomes. A richly detailed report is an essential requirement for qualitative researchers who, as a group, have been criticized for being unclear about research methodology. By seeking to make the research process transparent to the reader, we increase the likelihood that readers will seriously consider our work.

Lincoln and Guba (1985) describe several aspects of the research processes that contribute to trustworthiness, four of which are especially helpful for beginning qualitative researchers:

1 Multiple methods of data collection

The combination of interviews and observations from the field, along with reviews of relevant documents increases the likelihood that the phenomenon of interest is being understood from various points of view and ways of knowing. Convergence of a major theme or pattern in the data from interviews, observations and documents lends strong credibility to the findings.

2 Building an audit trail

By employing the methods for data collection and analysis we have described in this book, you will have a permanent *audit trail* of your research effort (Lincoln and Guba, 1985). The researcher's journal, the original interview transcripts and field notes, the unitized data, and the big paper process we describe and use as part of the constant comparative method of data analysis, all contribute to an audit trail. This documentation allows you to walk people through your work, from beginning to end, so that they can understand the path you took and judge the trustworthiness of your outcomes.

3 Working with a research team

Qualitative researchers who work alone often find their research criticized for being biased. In fact, much qualitative research is criticized for this reason; studies with nonmathematical results are suspect in a society that holds the dominant paradigm as paramount. If you work alone but use multiple methods and maintain an audit trail, you lay the foundation for a credible study. You can increase the trustworthiness of your work, however, if you work with others. A few human instruments working together are better than one. More specifically, team members act as 'peer debriefers', keeping each other honest (Lincoln and Guba, 1985). This peer debriefing function can also be done by an outside person who agrees to walk through your audit trail periodically, raising questions of bias when necessary.

4 Member checks

Lincoln and Guba (1985) use this term to refer to the process of asking research participants to tell you whether you have accurately described their experience. Have you produced a 'recognizable reality', in their view? Qualitative researchers have various opinions and practices regarding member checks, from listening to participants but not necessarily changing their results, to agreeing not to publish anything that the participants do not find truthful. We have found that members' feedback is very valuable and sometimes helps us see or emphasize something we missed. Most often we have found that people are surprised at how much or how succinctly their experience has been described, even in small intense studies of relatively short duration. In any case, all research participants appreciate and deserve to learn of the outcomes of a study they have helped make happen. The longitudinal study of girls' development by Brown and Gilligan (1992) provides an excellent description of how the researchers invited the girls to review and critique the research of which they were the focus.

Elliot Mischler has made a valuable contribution to the topic of trustworthiness in qualitative research. He advocates the practice of making research methodology visible for many of the reasons we discuss above, but he also proposes that the ultimate test of the trustworthiness of a qualitative study is whether we believe the findings strongly enough to act on them. In Mischler's words, 'the key issue becomes whether the relevant community of scientists evaluates reported findings as sufficiently trustworthy to rely on them for their own work' (1990: 417). We would expand Mischler's criteria for trustworthiness to include readers who are not scientists, but who find a research study so compelling, so filled with 'truth value' that they are willing to act on it outside the realm of social research. The research on women's ways of knowing by Belenky and her colleagues is an example of this larger criteria of trustworthiness (Belenky, Clinchy, Goldberger and Tarule, 1986). Not only have numerous studies followed on the heels of their work, but at least one women's college has gone so far as to reconstruct their college curriculum based on the uncovering of alternative ways of learning and knowing reported in the book (Vidulich, 1992). Without the rich detail contained in their research report, it is unlikely that other researchers and practitioners would have acted on the knowledge contained within it.

Note

1   We prefer to use the cut-and-paste method of preparing data for analysis, which results in data cards that are easy to manipulate. There are several computer programs, such as Ethnograph and LISQUAL, that are designed to assist in the process of analyzing qualitative data. However, we have found the more hands-on approach helpful for learning to do data analysis and for being able to visually pore over a large amount of data simultaneously.

References

BELENKY, M.F., CLINCHY, B.M., GOLDBERGER, N.R. and TARULE, J.M. (1986) *Women's Ways of Knowing: The Development of Self, Voice and Mind*, New York: Basic Books.

BLUMER, H. (1969) *Symbolic Interactionism: Perspectives and Method*, Englewood Cliffs, NJ: Prentice-Hall.

BOGDAN, R. and BIKLEN, S.K. (1982) *Qualitative Research for Education*, Boston, MA: Allyn and Bacon.

BROWN, L.M. and GILLIGAN, C. (1992) *Meeting at the Crossroads: Women's Psychology and Girls' Development*, Cambridge, MA: Harvard University Press.

GLASER, B.G. and STRAUSS, A.L. (1967) *The Discovery of Grounded Theory*, Chicago, IL: Aldine.

GOERTZ, J.P. and LeCOMPTE, M.D. (1981) 'Ethnographic research and the problem of data reduction', *Anthropology and Education Quarterly*, **12**, pp. 51–70.

GUBA, E.G. (1981) 'Criteria for assessing the trustworthiness of naturalistic inquiries', *Educational Communications and Technology Journal*, **29**, pp. 75–92.

KIDDER, L.H. (1981) 'Qualitative research and quasi-experimental frameworks', in BREWER, M.B. and COLLINS, B.E. (Eds) *Scientific Inquiry and the Social Sciences*, San Francisco, CA: Jossey-Bass.

LINCOLN, Y. and GUBA, E. (1985) *Naturalistic Inquiry*, Beverly Hills, CA: Sage.

MARSHALL, J. (1981) 'Making sense as a personal process', in REASON, P. and ROWAN, J. (Eds) *Human Inquiry: A Sourcebook of New Paradigm Research*, New York: John Wiley.

MAYKUT, P., ANDERSON, T., BERGDAHL, D., BRAUN, A., BRIGSON, B., DOHERTY, D.,

EFFLAND, B., HAINES, J., HIGHTOWER, M., HOGAN, S., KINGSLAND, D., PLOOR, W., PRIEBE, C., and WIDNER, M. (1991). *Experiences of college teaching: Beliefs and practices among instructors at a small private college.* Unpublished manuscript.

MAYKUT, P., BOUCHER, M., DOMBROWSKI, J., EHERENMAN, A., HUBBARD, J., LINK, T., LUND, C., OLSTAD, G., REIGEL, M., and YUE, H.S. (1992). *An exploration of young adults' experience of opposite-sex friendships.* Unpublished manuscript.

MAYKUT, P.S., BALTZ, A.M., BONDOW, K., BRAGUE, J., CLARK, R., HARRISON, A., JUNE, J., MCDONAH, J., MARTINE, A., PREMO, M., SCHNEIDER, L. and SERVAIS, J. (1992) *Reflections of Older Adults: Interim Report of Research Findings*, Unpublished manuscript.

MILES, M.B. and HUBERMAN, A.M. (1984) *Qualitative Data Analysis: A Sourcebook of New Methods*, Beverly Hills, CA: Sage.

MISCHLER, E.G. (1990) 'Validation in inquiry-guided research: The role of exemplars in narrative studies', *Harvard Educational Review*, **60**, pp. 415–42.

PATTON, M.Q. (1990) *Qualitative Evaluation and Research Methods* (2nd ed.), Newbury Park, CA: Sage.

SIBBET, D. (1981) *Workbook/Guide to Group Graphics*, San Francisco, CA: Graphic Guides, Inc.

STRAUSS, A. and CORBIN, J. (1990) *Basics of Qualitative Research: Grounded Theory Procedures and Techniques*, Newbury Park, CA: Sage.

TAYLOR, S.T. and BOGDAN, R. (1984) *Introduction to Qualitative Research Methods: The Search for Meanings* (2nd ed.), New York: Wiley.

VIDULICH, D. (1992, October) 'Women's ways of learning turn classes into quests', *National Catholic Reporter*, p. 5.

Chapter 10

Communicating the Outcomes of Qualitative Research

Academic journals and both popular and academic presses have acknowledged the value of the alternate paradigm and qualitative research by publishing considerably more qualitative research over the past two decades. Many scholars have called for the use of qualitative research to help us increase our understanding of human experience that heretofore has been limited by an adherence to the dominant paradigm and traditional methods of inquiry (Blieszner and Adams, 1992; Dornbusch, Petersen and Hetherington, 1991). Increasingly, intellectual space is being made available for communicating the outcomes of qualitative inquiry.

In previous chapters we have introduced you to several qualitative research reports presented in book form, such as William Perry's (1970) early study of college men's intellectual development, Mary Belenky and her associates' research on women's personal and intellectual development (Belenky, Clinchy, Goldberger and Tarule, 1986), Lyn Mikel Brown and Carol Gilligan's (1992) longitudinal case study research on girls' psychological development, and Heewon Chang's (1992) study of life in a US high school. Reading several research reports is essential preparation for writing and reveals the variety in style and format. Overall, these reports are rich in the reporting of actual data, particularly verbatim excerpts from in-depth interviews, which are interwoven into and illuminate the discussion of research findings.

But even book-length research reports require that researchers pare down discussions, highlighting the most prominent findings and selecting the data that best illustrates these findings. This task is even more challenging for researchers who submit their work to professional journals which have traditionally published more circumscribed research reports based on quantitative data. Increasingly, qualitative research reports in shortened form have appeared in professional journals and have been presented at professional conferences. The diversity of presentation modes for qualitative research reminds us that, as in all writing, we must decide the format and the audience for whom we write.

In this chapter we present a method for communicating your research methodology and outcomes in writing and in oral presentations. This method for organizing your writing can be used for book length or journal length reports, although we suggest that beginning researchers prepare a shorter manuscript that could be submitted for publication to a professional journal. The length of published qualitative research articles (that are not monographs) ranges from about twelve to twenty-five pages. The study of high school students at risk of dropping out of school by Farrell and his associates, described at length in an earlier chapter, is a useful example of a short research report (Farrell, Peguero, Lindsey and White, 1988). An example of the longer article is Douglas Biklen's narrative account of his research on the use of facilitated communication by people with autism (Biklen, 1990). The demands and possibilities of a book length manuscript will become evident in the process of writing a shorter report.

While we are not advocating a lock-step technique, we have seen the value in giving beginning researchers more than general suggestions for how to go about the hard task of writing up one's work. The method we describe assumes the researcher has followed the qualitative research approach presented in the previous chapters, particularly the use of the constant comparative method of data analysis and the development of propositions. We consider our approach to writing up qualitative research a modified case-study approach, combining several traditionally used sections on methodology with an extended discussion of the sample and the research outcomes. This same general approach is also useful for oral presentations of qualitative research, which may or not require a more lengthy written account. In either case, the process of carefully organizing your work for others will engage you in an intensive review of the people, settings, and information you have already labored over and learned from. New discoveries are possible, even likely, even at this point in the research process!

Getting Started

Many qualitative researchers believe that one should begin writing early in the process of conducting inquiry. The process of writing about a project requires additional analytical work and for many researchers this form of analysis-through-writing can clarify emerging themes and patterns, and provide leads to follow in subsequent data collection efforts. At the very least, some beginning writing can sensitize you to the language of the research participants and increase your familiarity with the data. These early pieces of writing may eventually find a place in your final report.

Certainly if you have prepared a proposal prior to beginning your research, it includes important information for your final report: the problem statement can become the basis for your introduction, and the methods section can be expanded to include the details of your final sample and data collection process. The sections of an article-length research report, we suggest, closely follow the guidelines of the *Publication Manual of the American Psychological Association* (APA) (1983). In addition to psychology, professional journals in the physical and health sciences, and other social sciences rely on the APA style guidelines for manuscripts submitted for publication. While we recognize the awkward fit of these guidelines and terminology for writing up qualitative research studies, the APA guidelines provide a useful and familiar place to begin. We suggest the following sections or some variation of them be included in a report, particularly if you plan to submit your manuscript to a professional journal:

- Abstract
- Introduction
- Research Design
  - •• Provisions for trustworthiness
- Methods
  - •• Sample
  - •• Data collection methods
  - •• Data analysis procedures
- Outcomes
- Implications
- References
- Appendix

Each of these sections will be discussed briefly below.

Abstract

An abstract is a concise summary of your research that describes your focus of inquiry, research design, methods and outcomes. It is usually about 100 words (APA, 1983). Whether you are planning to present your work orally or in writing, an abstract is both helpful to the reader and often required. Preparing the abstract after you have written your report is a helpful exercise requiring the skill of being both informative and brief. You can provide a helpful service to others by stating in your abstract that you have conducted a qualitative research study, a fact which is missing in many qualitative research abstracts. Currently it is difficult to identify studies that are qualitative in design by the abstract and title alone, prohibiting easy search for people interested in such work.

Introduction

Present the purpose of your research project, providing the reader with some context for understanding the relevance of your project. Related research, particularly other qualitative research, is important to discuss here. Include a succinct statement of your focus of inquiry, presented as either a statement or a question.

Research Design

We suggest separating research design from the methods section in order to highlight the use of the alternate paradigm and a qualitative research approach. Drawing again from your proposal, include a brief description of this approach and why you chose to use it. Describe in more specific terms your use of an emergent design case-study approach or a nonemergent design case-study approach. If you used the former, tell the reader what you specified before the study began and what emerged in the process of ongoing data collection and analysis. We have noticed that many qualitative research reports do not include a concise statement about the research design and it is left up to the reader to infer what has been done.

Provisions for trustworthiness

We also suggest that researchers include in the section on research design a discussion of their *provisions for trustworthiness*, which we discussed in the previous chapter. Inform the reader of the ways in which you planned for a rigorous credible exploration of your focus of inquiry.

Methods

As in all reports of research it is imperative that you lay out before the reader the process by which you arrived at your findings. The discussion of methods in explicit and understandable terms is sorely lacking from much of the reported qualitative research literature. This omission of rich methodological detail leaves the reader guessing about the particulars of what was done with whom and where, and for how long. The credibility of one's work in large part depends on a thorough discussion of one's research methodology. You want to help readers follow the audit trail you have established by your careful work, leading them to the outcomes you have derived with the sense that, 'Of course. I can see how this researcher arrived at these outcomes.' We suggest a set of subheadings for the methods section of the report that will be familiar to many readers.

Sample

In carrying out your research you may have focused on people's experiences through interviewing and observing, or focused on settings as your unit of analysis. As the term *case-study approach* suggests, you have studied one or more of these cases — people or settings — in your sample, and you will be describing these cases at some length. Your description of the sample should include detailed information on how you built your sample: 1) initial selection criteria for people or settings and subsequent changes in this criteria if the sample was part of an emergent research design (i.e., how were the participants or settings similar or homogeneous?); 2) procedure for achieving maximum variation within the sample (i.e., how were the people or settings different or heterogeneous?); and 3) how you gained access to these people or settings, including problems you may have encountered in building your sample.

This section of your report should also include a rich description of the people or settings that participated in your study. Pseudonyms are used for people and places, and any other identifying information is changed to ensure the confidentiality of the research participants. For journal length reports these descriptions are essentially thumbnail sketches of the participants, which would be expanded for a book length report or if there is only one 'case,' as in life history research. In either format, however, the information that is provided about the participants or settings should be that which is relevant to the focus of inquiry, rather than some standard set of sociodemographic descriptors. For example, in one student's study of Catholic lay persons' faith-related experiences and behaviors, the sample section included information about each participants' history of involvement with institutional religion, succinctly summarized (Hogan, 1993).

Data collection methods

In this section you want the reader to gain a strong sense of the rationale for the selection of the particular data collection procedures you chose; if and why those procedures changed or expanded if you employed an emergent research design; and how you went about doing what you did. Again, this critical process is vaguely presented in many qualitative research reports, an unfortunate practice for reasons already discussed. A well-described account of the researcher's journey engages readers and invites them to travel with you to the discussion of research outcomes.

For many years experimental researchers working from the assumptions of the dominant paradigm have been aware of *reactivity*, the term used to describe the unintended effects of the researcher on the outcomes of the study. In experimental research design, researchers attempt to control for this effect. The alternate paradigm assumes reactivity in a sense: the knower and the known are interdependent (Postulate II) and events are mutually shaped (Postulate IV). In addition, a key characteristic of qualitative inquiry is that the researcher functions as *the* data collection instrument, the human-as-instrument, to use Lincoln and Guba's (1985) term. Thus, it is imperative that qualitative researchers include themselves in a discussion of the data collection procedures. We suggest at minimum a reporting of gender and personal or professional information relevant to the phenomenon under study. In the student research study cited above, Hogan (1993) was herself a practicing member of the Catholic Church, a fact that was included in her report. In studies involving a research team, information about team members needs to be equally explicit.

Data analysis procedures

There are a variety of approaches to analyzing qualitative data. In the previous chapter we described a procedure known as the constant comparative method, originally introduced by Glaser and Strauss (1967) and later expanded by Lincoln and Guba (1985). Whether you have used this method or some other approach in your research, readers are again benefitted by an explicit and concise discussion of the procedure. While others have argued that the need for this kind of detailed information about qualitative methods is past (Wolcott, 1990), we have found otherwise. There is still a role for educating others, including other researchers, about the process of qualitative inquiry.

Overall, we encourage researchers to be transparent in the discussion of methods, revealing in essential detail what they did and why, in order to increase the trustworthiness of their work and people's knowledge about qualitative research. Preparation of a draft of one's introduction and methods sections can be a way of making clear progress on the report writing task, and allow you to focus your efforts on the main part of the research report: the outcomes.

Outcomes

We will discuss in some detail below how researchers can go about presenting the outcomes of their research. We include this section here since it is a separate part of the report, which combines what traditionally has been called the results and discussion sections. We think that a renaming of this part of the report can be helpful in alerting the reader to a different type of discussion, one that involves themes and patterns rather than statistical results. Related research is often integrated into this discussion.

Implications

We suggest that all researchers respond in writing to this important question about their work: 'So what?' Qualitative researchers contribute to knowledge through an accumulation of case-study research reports that extend or challenge earlier work. It is the responsibility of the researcher to participate in this discussion by relating his or her own work to previous research, suggesting specific directions for future research efforts and discussing the implications of the outcomes for practice, if appropriate.

References

A complete listing of works cited in the report is included in the reference list.

Appendix

One of the most frequently included items in an appendix for a qualitative research report is an interview schedule (see, for example, Belenky *et al.*, 1986; Meldman, 1987). Book length reports are more likely to include other documentation that helps the reader understand the research than one will find in an article length report.

Our list of sections for a qualitative research report is meant to serve as a guide; it is a close but not perfect fit for many current journals. Each professional journal has its own publication requirements and guidelines which researchers must pay careful attention to in order to increase the likelihood of finding their work in print.

Presenting the Outcomes

It is at this point in the writing process that we find the words of two authors poignant: British author Gene Fowler was once quoted as saying 'Writing is easy; all you do is sit staring at a blank sheet of paper until the drops of blood form on your forehead.' In a speech at the University of Wisconsin-LaCrosse, in October, 1992, author Kurt Vonnegut candidly commented on the writing process: '[Writing] is physically unpleasant. Your body doesn't want to sit still that long. Most people don't want to be alone that much.' Both authors point to the fact that writing is hard work. While this may appear to be an obvious point, we have found that beginning qualitative researcher-writers frequently think that because the process is long and difficult, they are doing something wrong. A qualitative research report, particularly because of the demands of the outcomes section, is likely to take considerably more time than the report for a quantitative research study. One's analytic work is still to be completed in the organization and writing of the outcomes.

In some ways, however, we have it better than the fiction writer. If we have done good work, the collaborators in our research effort, the people we have spoken to and the settings we have observed have yielded a rich body of information for us to analyze and present. If you have followed the data analysis process described in the previous chapter you already have several outcome propositions that form the bare bones outline of your outcomes section. If you have carefully maintained an audit trail by systematically coding your data to the categories you identified in the data, you also have the direct quotations or field note excerpts that you will select to illustrate your outcomes. Our subsequent discussion assumes you have done this work.

Prioritizing outcomes

Returning to the metaphor of the accordion for this discussion, recall that in the process of data analysis you pulled apart the data like the bellows of an accordion, identifying each salient category contained within it. For each category you formulated a propositional statement, a factual statement conveying the meaning of the data cards comprising each category. Next, you engaged in a kind of synthesis as you studied your propositions for possible connections to each other, finding patterns and relationships across propositions, bringing the meaning in the data into closer harmony. The result of this synthesis is a set of *outcome propositions* to be communicated in your report.

The first step in organizing for writing is to prioritize your outcome propositions by considering their importance in contributing to one's focus of inquiry and their prominence in the data. For example, we recently conducted a study of young adults' experience of opposite-sex friendships (Maykut *et al.*, 1993). Here, opposite-sex friendship refers to a close relationship between a woman and a man that is described by both people as a friendship, and in which there is no romantic or sexual involvement, i.e., they are not each other's girlfriend or boyfriend, nor are they dating. There is relatively little qualitative research on people's experience of opposite-sex friendships, but some survey research indicates that romantic or sexual attraction is experienced differently by men and women in this type of friendship. Rose (1985) reported that young adult men were motivated by sexual attraction to initiate opposite sex friendships, whereas the women were not. Our work suggested otherwise for the pairs we interviewed. A prominent outcome in the research was the experience of sexual attraction for both women and men toward their opposite-sex friend, and the management of this attraction for the good of the friendship (Maykut *et al.*, 1993). While this experience was not discussed by every member of every pair we interviewed, it was discussed by many, and thus was a prominent outcome of the study, adding to our understanding of young adults' experience of opposite-sex friendships.

Selecting representative excerpts from the data

You will not be able to write *ad infinitum* about everything revealed in your research study; prioritizing for relevance and prominence is critical. Once you have established an order of importance for presenting your outcomes, you are faced with the task of *how* to present these to the reader with the rich detail that characterizes qualitative research and the case-study approach. We suggest that you read through each of the data cards that have contributed to each outcome proposition to identify quotations from interviews or excerpts from field notes that best illustrate each proposition. Using a highlighting marker, for each outcome proposition select and highlight 3–5 excerpts from your data. You will then be able to draw on these selected excerpts for your report writing. Of course the context for each of these excerpts will be important, so have the original transcripts and field notes available for reference as you write. With the most relevant and prominent outcomes identified and the data that best illustrates these outcomes selected, you are almost ready to write.

Organizing the outcomes section

The outcomes of qualitative research, whether presented in article length or book length form, vary considerably in how they are organized depending in large part on the focus of inquiry and the sample. For example, if the researcher has studied one case in depth — one person or one setting — the report will often be organized by the overarching themes that have emerged from the study of that one person or place (see, for example, Bogdan, 1974). If the researcher has studied several people or settings, the report may be organized around each person or place, or by the themes that emerged across people or settings, or some combination of the two (see Farrell *et al.*, 1988; Koegel and Edgerton, 1984). It is also possible to find a qualitative research report that does not follow any of these formats (see Biklen, 1990).

We suggest that as a way of beginning the task of writing about one's outcomes, it often works to organize the outcomes section around the outcome propositions. Decide on a meaningful sequence for these propositions with the accompanying data excerpts to draw from while you write. Because you have previously described the sample (people or settings) in some depth, you will be able to refer to them in your discussion of the outcomes.

Writing the outcomes section

Finally the task is to weave together the outcome propositions and illustrative data into an interesting and informative narrative. You want people's thoughts, feelings and experiences to be conveyed in their own words whenever possible, while recognizing that report length is limited. Wolcott (1990) notes that the real challenge for qualitative re-searchers is deciding what *not* to include in their reports, referring both to the mound of data one has accumulated and the tendency for many of us to write more, when less will suffice. For example, as your report takes shape you may find that you need to 'talk' less and let the research participants talk more, or that less prominent outcomes can be discussed more briefly.

In weaving together the outcomes section, one's basic writing skills come strongly into play, and many of the oft-heard guides for writing apply; in particular: write first, edit later; minimize jargon; use the active voice; avoid sexist language. For the qualitative researcher the rich detail of human experience that he has discovered or uncovered must be conveyed to the reader, in contrast to the technical, almost terse, style of quantitative research reports. Share drafts of your work with friends who will give you frank feedback on both the substantive content of your research and on the mechanics of your writing.

In addition to the outcomes, we want to integrate into our discussion relevant information from other research studies, if available, to give a broader context to our work. Be sure to note whether the other research cited is qualitative or quantitative, keeping in mind the different paradigmatic assumptions that undergird each of these research approaches. We would not necessarily expect comparable findings. The integration of relevant research into the substance of the outcomes section can often be done after much of the section has been initially drafted. Relevant research is also likely to be further discussed in the implications section of the report.

Generating a Team's Research Report

Throughout the book we have encouraged the research team approach to conducting qualitative research. If you have worked as a team, you want to figure out ways to prepare your report that involves each team member. We have found it helpful to work closely as a group in the process of prioritizing propositions and selecting illustrative excerpts for each outcome from the data. The actual writing of the report can sometimes be divided up by sections, depending on the number of team members. We have found it useful to have one or two team members write a draft of the introduction, research design, and methods section, and one or two team members prepare a draft of the outcomes section. All team members provide feedback on the drafts, then discuss and write down implications and then divide up the work for the final copy. An alternative to dividing up the sections of the report is to have one team member do the writing, with team members offering feedback on drafts. This process relies heavily on the skills and interest of one team member and needs to be carefully negotiated by the team. However a team chooses to prepare its report, it is important that the final product be experienced by the team members as the result of their collective work.

Other Ways of Communicating Your Research

While it is true that writing is the primary mode for presenting one's research, there are alternative ways of communicating research that can add to or even substitute for a written report. Much qualitative research focuses on people's words, their thoughts, perceptions, attitudes, and experiences that can come to life when their words are read aloud. With a large group of graduate students we explored the school climate of our college by conducting in-depth interviews with students, faculty, administrators, housekeepers, janitors and other nonteaching staff. The outcomes of hundreds of hours of interviewing and data analysis were presented at a public meeting of the college community, with specific invitations to people who participated in the interviews. The student researchers presented the focus of inquiry and methods, wrote out the outcome propositions on large easels, and read aloud excerpts from the interviews that pointedly illustrated each outcome. Most of the research participants sitting in the audience heard some of their own words spoken. The language they heard was clearly the local language of this region and from a college community. Members of the audience squirmed when they heard *out loud* that while people who were interviewed perceived the faculty, overall, as 'very competent', they also saw some 'deadwood' on the faculty that diminished the generally positive school climate. The audience smiled knowingly at the finding that people 'cared about each other' at this small college. At the end of the presentation several members of the audience stated that they thought the research team had captured the school's climate, which added credibility to the research. For this study and its purpose, the oral presentation of the research outcomes worked effectively.

There are other ways of publicly presenting your research. We have used slides, taken throughout the course of a project, to illustrate the research process to audiences that are unfamiliar with qualitative research. Presenting one's work at a poster session, where many researchers simultaneously display key features of their work on posters and talk with interested people about it, can also be an effective means of communication. Overall, we encourage researchers to consider the many possible forums for presentation of their research, which will in turn help more of us to understand the process and the possibilities of a qualitative approach to understanding human experience.

References

AMERICAN PSYCHOLOGICAL ASSOCIATION (1983) *Publication Manual of the American Psychological Association* (3rd ed.), Washington, DC: Author.

BELENKY, M.F., CLINCHY, B.M., GOLDBERGER, N.R. and TARULE, J.M. (1986) *Women's Ways of Knowing: The Development of Self, Voice and Mind*. New York: Basic Books.

BIKLEN, D. (1990) 'Communication unbound: Autism and praxis', *Harvard Educational Review*, **60**, pp. 291–314.

BLIESZNER, R. and ADAMS, R.G. (1992) *Adult Friendship*, Newbury Park, CA: Sage.

BOGDAN, R. (1974) *Being Different: The Autobiography of Jane Frye*, New York: Wiley.

BROWN, L.M. and GILLIGAN, C. (1992) *Meeting at the Crossroads: Women's Psychology and Girls' Development*, Cambridge, MA: Harvard University Press.

CHANG, H. (1992) *Adolescent Life and Ethos: An Ethnography of a US High School,* London: Falmer Press.

DORNBUSCH, S.M., PETERSEN, A.C. and HETHERINGTON, E.M. (1991) 'Projecting on the future of research on adolescence', *Journal of Research on Adolescence*, **1,** pp. 7–17.

FARRELL, E., PEGUERO, G., LINDSEY, R. and WHITE, R. (1988) 'Giving voice to high school students: Pressure and boredom, "ya know what I'm sayin?" ' *American Educational Research Association*, **25**, pp. 489–502.

GLASER, B. and STRAUSS, A. (1967) *The Discovery of Grounded Theory*, Chicago, IL: Aldine.

HOGAN, S. (1993, May) A qualitative study of people's faith experiences and faith behaviors, paper presented at the Annual Spring Psychology Symposium, Viterbo College, LaCrosse, WI.

KOEGEL, P. and EDGERTON, R.B. (1984) 'Black "six-hour retarded children" as young adults', in EDGERTON, R.B. (Ed) *Lives in Process: Mildly Retarded Adults in a Large City* Washington, DC: American Association on Mental Deficiency, pp. 145–171.

LINCOLN, Y.S. and GUBA, E.G. (1985) *Naturalistic Inquiry*, Beverly Hills, CA: Sage.

MAYKUT, P.S., BOUCHER, M., DOMBROSKI, J., EHERENMAN, A., HUBBARD, J., LINK, T., LUND, C., OLSTAD, G., REIGEL, M. and YUE, H.S. (1993) *An exploration of young adults' experience of opposite-sex friendships.* (unpublished manuscript).

MELDMAN, L.S. (1987) 'Diabetes as experienced by adolescents', *Adolescence*, **86**, pp. 433–44.

PERRY, W.G. (1970) *Forms of Intellectual and Ethical Development in the College Years: A Scheme*, New York: Holt, Rinehart and Winston.

ROSE, S.M. (1985) 'Same- and cross-sex friendships and the psychology of homosociality', *Sex Roles*, **12**, pp. 63–74.

WOLCOTT, H.F. (1990) *Writing up Qualitative Research*, Newbury Park, CA: Sage.

Appendix

Research Proposal I
submitted to the
School District of La Crosse
by
Richard Morehouse, Ph.D., and
Pam Maykut, Ph.D.
June, 1986

I. Definition of the Project
    A. Statement of the Proposed Project
        We have been interested in working with a school that would
        like to find out what parents think and feel about a topic or
        an issue that is of concern to the school — teachers and/or
        administrators. Our goal is to provide summer session graduate
        students, all of whom are experienced teachers, with an op-
        portunity to engage in an actual qualitative* research study.

        We approached Glen Jenkins, principal of Longfellow
        Middle School with our ideas. He was very interested in the
        project and identified a topic area to be explored with parents:
        'School Climate'. We are proposing a study of parent
        perspectives on the school climate of Longfellow School, based
        on in-depth interviews with interested parents. The interviews
        would take place the week of June 13, 1988.

        [*a research model that is primarily exploratory and descrip-
        tive, and for which people's words and actions are the main
        source of data.]
    B. Brief History of the Problem
        We have been informed by Glen Jenkins that there has been
        considerable interest in 'school climate', beginning with the
        reorganization of the middle schools in 1980. We understand
        that several district administrators, including Jenkins, were

involved in in-service training on school climate about that time. In addition, Jenkins was a member of the survey team that conducted a School Climate Mini-Audit of Longfellow Middle School in February, 1981. (Jenkins was principal of another school at the time of the audit.) Jenkins, now the principal of Longfellow School, has addressed many of the concerns related to school climate raised in the mini-audit. He has invited us, with the permission of the school district, to interview interested parents about the school climate of Longfellow School.

C.   Definition of Terms or Concepts

'School climate' is a term that has been used to describe the activities, processes, and projects of a school that contribute to how people think and feel about the school (Boise *et al.*, 1975; Smith *et al.*, 1978). A positive school climate is characterized by caring, trusting, cohesiveness, respect, high morale, school renewal, and continuous academic and social growth. Indices of a positive school climate include such things as a small number of discipline problems, absence of vandalism, high percentage of attendance, a low drop-out rate, and people talking to one another with courtesy, among other things.

Determinants of school climate have been grouped into three major areas: program determinants, process determinants, and material determinants. Program determinants of a positive school climate include such things as the opportunities for active learning, individualized performance expectations, and varied learning environments. Process determinants of a positive school climate include such things as problem-solving ability, effective communications, and effective teaching-learning strategies (Boise *et al.*, 1975). Program and process determinants, in particular, have been identified by Jenkins as areas that he would like parents to comment on.

D.   Hypothesis

The proposed project is designed to explore the topic of school climate of Longfellow School with parents. Therefore, there is no specific hypothesis being tested. Rather, the interview is designed to allow parents to discuss what is most salient for them, within the context of a semi-structured interview schedule on school climate.

II.   Design of the Project

A.   *Proposed starting/ending dates*: On school district form

B.   *Extent of school personnel involved*: On school district form

C. *Instrumentation*: Attached is a copy of the interviewer's form of the *Longfellow School Climate Interview: Parent Perspectives*

D. Procedures for data collection

    1. Parents of students at Longfellow School will receive the school *Newsletter* containing a notice about the project and a form for indicating their interest, to be returned to the school.

    2. Principal will notify Viterbo researchers of interested parents. Parents will then receive a letter of confirmation as to the date, time, location of the interview, and the name of the graduate student who will be interviewing them. [Graduate students will receive in-class instruction and rehearsal on conducting interviews.]

    3. Parents will be interviewed on either June 13 and June 14, 1988. Interviews will last approximately one-and-a-half hours, and will be tape recorded unless parents object.

    4. Tape-recorded interviews will be transcribed and analyzed by students.

    5. Outcomes of the study will be presented to interested school and district administrators, and interested parents.

III. Method of Evaluation for the Project

    A. Evaluation of usefulness to Longfellow School and La Crosse School District

Jenkins has stated that the results of the school climate study will be used in developing goals for Longfellow School. Thus, the study can be evaluated on the extent to which it yields information that is useful for goal development.

Second, parents will be invited to hear the results of the study in which they participated. From a qualitative research perspective, it is important that researchers present their findings to participants, in order that they may determine whether the researchers have portrayed a 'recognizable reality' (Entwistle, 1984). To the extent that we are able to present a 'recognizable reality' to parents, our project will be successful.

In addition, the implementation of the proposed project, i.e., outreach to parents, may result in increased linkages between parents and the school.

    B. Evaluation of usefulness to Viterbo College graduate students

Since the proposed project was initiated for the purpose of providing a real research opportunity to students, we will also be evaluating the experience based on our course goals.

IV. Significance of the Project
    A. For Longfellow School
        As stated above, it is Jenkins' expressed intention that the results of the study be used in developing goals for Longfellow School. In particular, study results will be used by the school's team leaders and school climate team in decision-making and goal development.
    B. For the School District of La Crosse
        Jenkins also indicated that results from the study may be useful in district-wide goal development.
    C. For Education in General
        We are particularly enthused about using qualitative research methodology in understanding educational programs and processes. Qualitative educational research is a mushrooming field of inquiry, and we believe we can contribute methods and ideas to this field through our experience with the proposed study.

References

BOISE, H.E., BRAINARD, E., FLETCHER, E., FOX, R.S., HUGE, J.S., OLIVERO, J.L., SCHMUCK, R., SHAHEEN, T.A. and STEGEMAN, W.H. (1975) *School Climate: A Challenge to the School Administrator*, Bloomington, IN: Phi Delta Kappa.

ENTWISTLE, N. (1984) 'Contrasting perspectives on learning', in MARTON, F., HOUNSELL, D. and ENTWISTLE, N. (Eds) *The Experience of Learning*, Edinburgh: Scottish Academic Press, pp. 1–18.

SMITH, R.M., NEISWORTH, J.T. and GREER, J.G. (1978) *Evaluating Educational Environments*, Columbus, OH: Charles E. Merril.

Research Proposal II
An Exploration of How Children and Adolescents with Autism or Autistic Tendencies Use Facilitated Communication in Their Lives submitted by Michelle Boucher and Cindy Lund, Viterbo College to Chileda Habilitation Institute, LaCrosse, Wisconsin
April 2, 1993

Problem Statement

The purpose of this study is to further understand how children and adolescents diagnosed with autism or autistic tendencies use facilitated communication in their lives. Our interest was spurred by reading qualitative studies on facilitated communication by Douglas Biklen of Syracuse University and Rosemary Crossley of the Dignity through Education and Language Communication Centre (DEAL) in Melbourne, Australia, and also by our own work at Chileda Habilitation Institute where several children and adolescents with autism reside.

Leo Kanner was the first to delineate the syndrome of early infantile autism. Of the eleven children he observed, he identified an 'inability to relate themselves in the ordinary way to people and situations from the beginning of life' (1943: 41). This inability to relate to the world seemed to be due to the fact these children experienced withdrawal, language difficulties, cognitive difficulties and behavioral problems. The major drawback of these characteristics is the fact that people with autism are not able to communicate or to understand the attempts by others to communicate with them.

According to Simons and Oishi, authors of *The Hidden Child: The Linwood Method for Reaching the Autistic Child*, 'communicative speech is an integral part of overall functioning in both normal and autistic children' (1987: 179). Those children who do have useful communicative abilities at about age five are more likely to improve than those with none (Schwartz and Johnson, 1981). Therefore, attempts have been made to help increase the ability of those with autism to express themselves effectively (Webster, Konstantareas, Oxman and Mack, 1980).

A first attempt was made through speech training, but this did not prove to be effective. The children responded more effectively to gestures made rather than to the spoken word (Konstantareas, Webster and Oxman, 1979). This discovery of the effectiveness of gestural communication led to attempts at simultaneous communication by Konstantareas and colleagues (Konstantareas, *et al.*, 1979). Simultaneous communication is the use of sign language and speech to communicate. Although sign language appears to be useful for expressing needs, it does not seem to be useful in actual conversational communication. According to Oxman, Webster, and Konstantareas, 'sign language training is not, of course, a panacea for severely dysfunctional, nonverbal children' (1978: 222).

These methods have been the main attempts at fostering communication, yet they are not effective for a broad scope of children with autism, namely those considered 'severely dysfunctional'. Therefore, a method has been sought which is more applicable to conversational communication and will be helpful even to those who have not responded to previous methods. Crossley (1992) and Biklen (1990) both claim that a new method called 'facilitated communication' has been effective with individuals described as 'severely intellectually disabled'. Cummins and Prior provide a useful definition of facilitated communication:

> [Facilitated communication is] a method of training people in the use of augmentative communication aids which involves the communication partner or facilitator, providing physical assistance to aid users to help them to overcome physical and emotional problems using their aid . . . The technique differs from graduated guidance in that the intention of movement is the responsibility of the message sender. The message receiver is making physical contact with the sender only to overcome or minimize psychoemotional and/or neurophysiological problems affecting access.
>
> (Cummins and Prior, 1992: 331)

Despite the effectiveness Crossley and Biklen claim facilitated communication has had, Crossley (1992) does admit that facilitated communication has not, as yet, been used with many children with autism. For people who have been introduced to facilitation, it has been effective, according to Biklen (1990). He has video-recorded children typing phrases on their augmentative communication aids such as, 'IM NOT RETARDED. MY MOTHER FEELS IM STUPID BECAUSE IH (backspaced and crossed out the "h") CANT USE MY VOICE PROPERLY' (Biklen, 1990: 296). The words and meaning expressed in this way by children have encouraged interest in understanding facilitated communication, though there has been relatively little empirical research to date.

There are several reasons why this method may be effective with children with autism. Showing by pointing to letters is the key to facilitated communication, rather than speaking or writing. For children with autism, pointing is one of the earliest symbolic gestures. Due to a lack of interest in speech, children with autism are less likely to respond to verbal prompts than physical prompts (Wing, 1976). Individuals with autism present symptoms that show a need for physical support to begin, follow through and stop some movements. Facilitated communication uses physical prompting. This physical prompting is more easily faded out over time than is verbal prompting (Donnellan, Sabin and Majure, 1992).

A second reason facilitated communication may be effective is that many individuals who are severely communicatively impaired are not as intellectually disabled as they have been presumed to be. In fact, out of 431 children who were severely communicatively impaired and over the age of five, 70 per cent showed useful literacy skills, defined as the ability to type a comprehensible sentence without a model (Crossley, 1992). This shows that assumptions have been incorrect in the past; people with autism may not be as intellectually disabled as earlier research and practice indicated.

A final reason to examine the lives of people using facilitated communication is that previous attempts for communication have not been as successful as desired. Two-thirds of the DEAL clients diagnosed as autistic had exposure to manual signing and only four had acquired more than 100 signs. By comparison, facilitated communication has been much more effective (Crossley, 1992).

Focus of Inquiry

It is necessary to further examine the role facilitated communication has played in the lives of children and adolescents with autism because at this time there is little information and empirical research on this topic. What is available focuses mainly on whether or not the method works. The focus of our inquiry is to understand how children and adolescents with autism or autistic tendencies are using facilitated communication in their lives.

Research Design

The topic we want to explore is best suited to a qualitative research approach. According to Lincoln and Guba the purpose of a qualitative study is to 'accumulate sufficient knowledge to lead to understanding' (1985: 227). They recommend the use of an emergent research design, which means that data collection and data analysis are simultaneous and ongoing activities that allow for important understandings to be discovered along the way and then pursued in additional data collection efforts. In an emergent research design, not all the specifics of a study can be outlined in advance. What we can specify ahead of time is presented below.

This qualitative approach to inquiry also involves a case-study approach, where people and settings are explored in depth and described in detail in the final report. We believe an emergent research design case-study approach will help us explore the lives of children and adolescents with autism or autistic tendencies who are using facilitated communication.

Provisions for trustworthiness

There are several things we have built into our research design that will increase the trustworthiness of our research. We will use several methods of data collection and several sources of information, and conduct data collection over a six-month period. We will be working in a two-person team, ensuring that a single researcher's bias is less likely. We have asked Dr. Pam Maykut to serve as our *peer debriefer* and regularly review our data analysis. Lastly, we will present our outcomes to the people who have participated in the research. We will ask them whether we have accurately captured at least some of the life experience of children and adolescents with autism or autistic tendencies who are using facilitated communication.

Methods

Sample

We would like to conduct our research with four of the young people currently living at Chileda Habilitation Institute. Using a purposive sampling approach, we will select the participants based on maximum variation among those children and adolescents at Chileda. The similarities of the participants will be that they have been diagnosed with autism or autistic-like characteristics, are under 19 years of age, and are currently using facilitated communication in their lives. The ways in which we would like to vary the participants are by: a) age; b) gender (although we realize that autism is more prevalent in boys); c) length of time residing at Chileda; and d) amount of exposure to facilitated communication, including the length of time using it and the number of facilitators. Our research may indicate that we need to include individuals who vary from each other in other ways, so we would like to have the option of expanding the size of the sample in the future, if we have the time and resources.

Methods of data collection

In our study we will use a variety of methods of data collection to achieve a better understanding of the participants, and to increase the credibility of our findings. As stated above, we will employ an emergent research design. This means that if we find other, possibly more substantial, ways of understanding the lives of the participants than those listed below, we will include them.

(a) Observations. We would like to observe the four participants in various aspects of their everyday lives, including observations of classroom work, recreational life, community outings, and any other appropriate times or places where the participants may use facilitated communication. We will take field notes during or after our observations, whichever is most appropriate.

(b) Interviews. One important way of understanding people's lives is to understand them through the eyes and voices of the prominent people in their lives. These are the people who have insights through knowing the child or adolescent well. These people would be the family and friends of the child. Also included in the circle would be teachers, child-care workers, and facilitators. Interviews with these prominent people will be done at their convenience. We will take notes

during or after the interviews, or ask for permission to audio-tape record long interviews, which will later be transcribed for use in data analysis.

(c) Review of documents. Lastly, we believe we can understand the lives of people with autism by reviewing charts which may be applicable to this understanding. We would like to review any documentation that may be helpful, such as notes, behavior documents, tests and texts from facilitation. We would review these with the intent of taking notes from them for analysis.

Confidentiality

We are very conscious of the rights of the children and adolescents who reside at Chileda. Names and places will be changed in our research report to protect the identity of the participants and their families. No information obtained during the course of the study will be discussed with anyone outside of the research team and peer debriefer without the written permission of the participants or their families.

Data Analysis

All field notes and transcripts from audio-taped interviews will be prepared for analysis by first photocopying all data, and then identifying *units of meaning* in the data. These units of meaning will then be separated and taped to 5″ x 8″ index cards for easy manipulation during data analysis.

We will be using the method known as the *constant comparative method* to analyze the data (Glaser and Strauss, 1967). This is a non-mathematical procedure that is designed to identify themes and patterns in qualitative data. We will systematically sort through the data we have collected. The research findings of this type of analysis can be presented in the form of propositions that summarize the salient themes and patterns within individual lives and across individuals' lives (Lincoln and Guba, 1985). The validity of such findings ultimately rests on whether the participants or people who know them will see a recognizable reality in these propositions.

Report of Outcomes

We will report our research outcomes to the children and adolescents who participated in the study, their families and Chileda staff. We will also prepare a formal report of our research to be submitted to our professor for class requirements.

References

BIKLEN, D. (1990) 'Communication unbound: Autism and praxis', *Harvard Educational Review*, **60**, pp. 291–313.

CROSSLEY, R. (1992, May) 'Lending a hand: A personal account of the development of facilitated communication training', *American Journal of Speech Language Pathology*, pp. 15–18.

CUMMINS, R.A. and PRIOR, M.P. (1992) 'Autism and assisted communication: A response to Biklen', *Harvard Educational Review*, **62**, pp. 228–41.

DONNELLAN, A.M., SABIN, L.A. and MAJURE, L.A. (1992, August) 'Facilitated communication: Beyond the quandary to the questions', *Topics in Language Disorders*, pp. 69–82.

GLASER, B.G. and STRAUSS, A.L. (1967) *The Discovery of Grounded Theory*, Chicago, IL: Aldine.

LINCOLN, Y.S. and GUBA., E.G. (1985) *Naturalistic Inquiry*, Beverly Hills, CA: Sage.

KANNER, L. (1943) 'Autistic disturbances of affective contact', in DONNELLAN, A.M. (Ed), *Classic Readings in Autism*, New York: Teachers College Press, pp. 217–50.

KONSTANTAREAS, N.M., WEBSTER, C.D. and OXMAN, J. (1979) 'An alternative to speech training: Simultaneous communication', in WEBSTER, C.D., KONSTANTAREAS, N.M., OXMAN, J. and MACK, J.E. (Eds) *Autism: New Directions in Research and Education*, New York: Pergamon Press, pp. 187–201.

OXMAN, J., WEBSTER, C.D. and KONSTANTAREAS, N.M. (1978) 'The perception and processing of information by severely dysfunctional and nonverbal children: A rationale for the use of gestural communication', in WEBSTER, C.D., KONSTANTAREAS, N.M., OXMAN, J. and MACK, J.E. (Eds) *Autism: New Directions in Research and Education*, New York: Pergamon Press, pp. 221–34.

SCHWARTZ, S. and JOHNSON, J.H. (1981) *Psychopathology of Childhood: A Clinical-experimental Approach*, New York: Pergamon Press.

SIMONS, J. and OISHI, S. (1987) *The Hidden Child: The Linwood Method for Reaching the Autistic Child*, Kensington, MA: Woodbine House.

WEBSTER, C.D., KONSTANTAREAS, N.M., OXMAN, J. and MACK, J.E. (1980) *Autism: New Directions in Research and Education*, New York: Pergamon Press.

WING, L. (1976) *Early Childhood Autism*, New York: Pergamon Press.

Interview Schedule
Television and Society:
Perspectives of Viterbo
College Students
Constructed by members of
Psychology 235

Introduction

- Who you are (interviewer)
- Name
- Describe your enrollment in Psych 235 — Qualitative Research Methods, and explain that the class is cooperatively engaged in a class research project. Note that you are working under the supervision of Drs. Maykut and Morehouse.
- Indicate that you are one of 14 student researchers who will be interviewing students from Viterbo College. Inform interviewer that she or he is one of approximately 14 students who will be interviewed.

Purpose of the study

The purpose of this study is to explore the role of television in the lives of students, and how they view the role of television in society. We are particularly interested in your perspectives and experiences, as they relate to your life as a student, in general, and as a member of a society in which television is ever-present.

The answers from all the people we interview will be combined into a summary that we will be sharing with Charles Kuralt, a CBS news reporter who will be visiting our campus in May. Mr.

Kuralt will be on campus for two days, and during that time our class is going to be talking with him about 'Television and Society'. We thought it would be important to find out what today's students have to say about television, and so we are conducting this study.

Tape recording, note taking, and confidentiality

Ask interviewee if you can tape record the interview. Let him/her know that it is important for you to 'capture' *their* words and ideas, and using the tape recorder will allow you to do this. Also ask if you can take some notes while you are conducting the interview, so that you can keep track of the interview as it progresses. [If the interviewee does not permit tape recording, take copious notes, and immediately reconstruct the interview afterward.]

Inform interviewees that nothing they say will ever be identified with them personally, and that they will not be identified by name as a study participant.

Turn on the Tape Recorder and test it together

- Why we are interviewing you:
  (a) You go to school here and you said 'yes!' OR
  (b) Someone (name _____) suggested you might be interested in being interviewed [if, in fact, this is the case].

A. Background [Questions without numbers are possible probes.]

A1. To start out, I'd like you to think about what stands out for you in your life since you became a student at Viterbo? What kinds of things have been important?
What stays with you?

A2. Tell me about what your life is like right now. Describe your life for me. [If interviewee focuses on television, listen, and then encourage description of a broader context].
What do you think about?
What do you care about?

A3. I'd be interested in knowing about the important relationships in your life right now. You don't need to identify people by name — just refer to individuals in a way that feels comfortable to you.

What makes each relationship important?

B. Past experiences related to television

B1. As I said at the beginning of the interview, we are interested in learning about the role of television in people's lives. Most of us have spent all or part of our lives with television sets around. When you think about what brought you to the TV as a child, what kind of things come to mind?

What were your favorite programs?

What was it about these shows that made them your favorites?

B2. What role did television viewing have in your family as you were growing up?

Physical location: Where was it, who sat where (Ask person to draw you a map.)

Use: Frequency, viewing times, programs viewed just by you, just by children, by whole family.

Rules: What rules did your family have for watching television — either *stated* or *unwritten rules?* How did the rules change as you got older?

B3. When you were a child, how did you decide what you were going to watch?

B4. What strong recollections do you have of particular shows, episodes, or moments you saw on TV as a child? [Try to elicit the content, and emotions associated with the content.]

C. Current television viewing (settings, behaviors, preferences)

C1. We've spent some time thinking back about television. Now I'd like you to come back to the present and think about your current television viewing. How would you describe yourself as a *viewer*?

What kind of viewer are you?

How would you characterize yourself as a viewer?

C2. Describe the place(s) where you are most likely to watch television.
Physical locations, actual layout of the rooms, where the TV is located in the room. [You could have interviewee draw you a map!]

C3. With whom are you most likely to watch? Individual names are not important — you can describe these people in terms of their relationship to you.

C4. What do you like to watch if you have time?

C5. Suppose I was with you while you were watching _____ [name some program mentioned by interviewee]. What would be going on?
Viewing behavior: level of attention, food, conversation, other activities while viewing; does viewing behavior change if program changes? if co-viewers change? if location changes?

C6. Describe for me, if you can, a typical viewing week — a non-exam week!
When, where, what, for how long?

C7. Now, if you can, I'd like you to try to reconstruct your television viewing over the past few days (or the last few days when the interviewee watched TV). What did you actually watch?
When, where, with whom?

C8. What things stand out for you from the television you watched over the past few days?

C9. What TV advertisements catch your attention? What is it that catches your attention?

C10. How do you decide what you are going to watch?

C11. Tell me about any recent conversations that you've had with others about television.
[Let interviewee describe conversations about TV in general, i.e., the influence of TV in our lives, or about specific conversations about particular programs, actors, plots, etc.]

C12. Is what you watch now different from what you watched five years ago? [If yes] In what way? What do you think accounts for this difference, for you?

D. Reflections on the influence of television

D1. You've told me some things about your current television viewing. I would like you to continue to reflect on your experience of television viewing. Our instructor told us that he learned about buttoning and unbuttoning his sports coat from watching Johnny Carson. Men are supposed to walk into a room with their coat buttoned and unbutton their coat before they sit down. Our instructor said that he became aware that he had learned this from the Carson show about ten years ago. *What are some things that you think you have learned from television?* Please take some time to think about this. What do you think is the most powerful thing you've learned from TV?
[If the interviewee has taken some time and cannot think of anything, fine. Perhaps he or she will think of something later.]

D2. What kinds of things do you *expect* to learn from television?
What kinds of things do you count on television for?

D3. Can you recall a recent program(s) that you had a strong emotional reaction to? [If yes] Please tell me about it.

D4. What do you think are the most powerful *messages* portrayed on television? [Note here that you are looking for what the interviewee believes are the basic themes communicated by what is shown on television.]
Taken together, all that you've watched and heard, what do you think are the strongest messages?

D5. Some people experience things they see on television as very real, and for other people, television is *un*real — it's made up. How about you?

D6. This may sound a little corny. Which television character do you think you are most like? What similarities do you share? [If interviewee says he/she is not like anyone, ask what makes him/her different from the characters portrayed on TV.]

D7. Of all the possible things that could be on TV, relatively few are shown. What are your impressions about how this selection process takes place?

How do you think this happens?
What do you think determines whether a certain program or topic is aired or not?

WE'RE ALMOST FINISHED! JUST A FEW MORE QUESTIONS.

E. Closing questions

E1. Summarize some of the things the interviewee has shared with you, e.g., 'You've told me quite a lot about what you think about your experience of different television programs, and also some of your thoughts about the power of television to influence society.' [*You come up with your own summary of some of the interviewee's points.*] Then ask this question: If you had the power to change the nature of television as we know it, what would you do?

E2. You may have heard people say that we are in the midst of an Information Age — an Age of Information. This characterization suggests that our society is changing in response to the vast amounts of information that we must deal with. If this is true, what do you think is the role of television in an Information Age?

E3. This last question may be difficult to answer, but I'd like to get your thoughts on it. You've told me that for all (or part) of your life you've had access to television. And you watched quite a bit (some, at least a little, etc., as it fits interviewee) of it growing up. How do you think you might be different today, if you had not had access to television as you were growing up?
[Give the interviewee time to think about this.]

E4. We're at the end of the interview now. Is there anything you would like to ask me?

E5. If possible, we may be going back to people that have been interviewed to ask them a few more questions. Would you be willing to talk with me again, only for a shorter period of time?
THANK YOU VERY MUCH FOR LETTING ME INTERVIEW YOU!

Interview Schedule[1]
Exploring People's Experience of Cross-sex Friendships Constructed by Members of Psychology 235: Qualitative Research Methods Viterbo College, Spring 1993

Introduction

- Who you are (interviewer)
    - Introduce yourself and describe your enrollment in Psychology 235: Qualitative Research Methods. Inform the interviewees that the class members are cooperatively engaged in this research project. Also inform the interviewees that you are under the supervision of Dr Pam Maykut.
    - Indicate that you are one of the student researchers who will be interviewing pairs of opposite-sex friends between the ages of 19–25. Inform interviewees that they are one of the nine pairs of opposite-sex friends who are being interviewed for the project.

- Purpose of the study
Share the purpose of the study with the interviewees:

    The purpose of this study is to learn more about people's experience of opposite-sex friendships, particularly among young adults. This is a relatively new area of research in psychology, and there is not a great deal of information on this particular type of friendship. There is also very little research that involves joint interviewing — bringing two people together to talk about a shared experience. We think that by conducting even this small study and by doing joint interviews we can learn some important things about the nature of opposite-sex friendships.

When we are done interviewing all the pairs of friends, we will be studying our interviews for common themes and patterns that might help us have a better understanding of opposite-sex friendships. We would like to share our findings with you. If you would like a copy of our report, please let me know. I will ask you about this again at the end of the interview.

- Why we are interviewing the two of you
  You two were asked to participate in the project because you describe yourselves as being friends who are not romantically involved with each other. We know, of course, that many people who are romantically involved also describe their partner as a friend, but we are not exploring that type of close relationship in this project.

- Confidentiality, tape recording, and note-taking
  Ask the interviewees if you can tape record the interview. Let them know that it is important for you to capture their words and ideas, and using the tape recorder will allow you to do this. Also let them know that you may take some notes while you are conducting the interview, so that you can keep track of the interview as it progresses.

  Inform the interviewees that they will not be identified or described in any way that would reveal their identity. Let them know that the interviews from the nine pairs will be studied by a group of student researchers, BUT that you will assign them pseudonyms (fake names) and change any information that would reveal who they are.

  You may also want to ask at this point: 'Are there any questions you would like to ask me before we get started?'

TURN ON THE TAPE RECORDER. Ask the interviewees if it is ok to tape record the interview. Record their verbally stated permission. Then rewind and *check* to be sure that the recording is satisfactory.

IF THE INTERVIEWEES REFUSE PERMISSION TO TAPE RECORD, take some notes while the interview proceeds, and immediately after the interview reconstruct as much of it as you can — their actual words and also your observations. You will also need to do this if your tape recording equipment breaks down.

*****INTERVIEW QUESTIONS*****

Additional instructions for interviewers are in brackets [   ].
Think of your own problems and write them in if it helps you.

Know your questions! Be curious!

A. General Questions on Friendship

A1.   Since this is a project about friendship, I'd like to start off with some general questions about friendship. What do you think are some characteristics of a good friendship?

[Seek responses from *both* people. Try not have the same person always respond first. Try to foster a conversation with a purpose.]

A2.   What qualities do you look for in a friend?

A3.   What creates a strong friendship?

A4.   [Have blank maps and markers/pens ready.] I'd be interested in learning about what might be called your 'friendship map'. One way to describe this group of people is by drawing a map.

[Give them the blank maps and also show them your own as an example.]

On this paper I'd like you to indicate the different people who you consider your friends, and to place them in the circle that reflects the closeness you feel with them. You do not need to name them for me. Just indicate them by an initial and whether they are a woman or man.

[Give interviewees ample time to each do their maps.]

A5.   Now I'd like you to each tell me about your map — talk me through it, if you would.

A6.   Now I'd like you to circle the person you would consider your 'best' or 'closest' friend.

A7.   For female: I notice that you have _____(#) men/guys that you consider friends. For male: I notice that you have _____(#) women/girls that you consider friends. In general, what difference do you each see between your friendships with people of the same sex, in comparison to your friendships with people of the opposite-sex?

[Use the interviewees' language as much as you can. For example, if they say 'guys', you say 'guys'.]

A8. What models of an opposite-sex friendship have you seen or known?

[Probe: What did they do? What did you see as valuable in these models?]

B. History of Their Friendship

B1. I'd like to hear about the history of *your* friendship. How did your friendship begin?

[Seek a rich description of the history of this friendship. Who? What? Where? When? How long?]

B2. What were your first impressions of each other?

B3. How have your first impressions changed as you have come to know each other better?

B4. What past experiences have you two shared that have really 'cemented' your relationship?

B5. What other events or experiences have been important in the development of your relationship?

C. Day-to-day Experience of the Friendship

C1. I'd like you to talk a little bit about the day-to-day nature of your friendship. What kind of things do you do together, when it's just the two of you?

[*Seek specific examples.* Tell me about some recent things that you have done together.]

C2. What type of things do you do when the two of you go out with a larger group of friends?

[*Seek specific examples.* Tell me about some recent things that you have done with friends.]

C3. How often do you actually get together, either the two of you or with a larger group of friends?

C4. How often do you talk to one another?

C5. When do you find yourselves communicating the most?

C6. What kind of things do you talk about with one another?

[*Seek specific examples.* Would you mind telling me about a few of your more recent conversations? What were they about?]

C7. Ask each: What things do you talk about with (*friend's name*) that you might not talk about with your same-sex friends?

C8: Now I'd like to ask you the reverse of that last question. Ask each: What things do you talk about with your same-sex friends that you might not talk about with (*friend's name*).

C8. Ask each: What kinds of new experiences or new people have come your way because of your friendship with (*friend's name*)?

C9. Most psychologist would argue that in all good relationships there is conflict. What kind of conflicts have the two of you had over the course of your friendship?

[Also probe for how they went about *resolving* the conflicts.]

D. How Each Sees the Other

D1. In this next part of the interview I am going to ask you to talk about each other. Ask each: How would you describe (*friend's name*) to someone who has never met her/him?

D2. Ask each: How do you describe your relationship with (*friend's name*) when other people ask about it?

D3. Ask each: What do you know about (*friend's name*) that very few other people probably know?

Note

1 The interview schedule developed for our project is actually somewhere between an interview schedule and an interview guide. Because of the size of our research team and our various skill levels, the detail provided in an interview schedule is useful. BUT you can use the questions provided or rephrase them in your own words *as long as you keep the intent of the*

question the same. You can use this sequence or skip around. You can go deeper into topics that seem important to understanding the experience of your pair. Your own skill and the 'conversational path' the interviewees take will determine the nature of the interview format and its content.

Index

abstract of reports 152–3
access, gaining, in research 70–2, 154
action and speech 18–19, 27–8, 35, 46, 47, 68, 128
Adams, R.G. 150
Ainsworth, M. 8
Allport, G.W. 111
ambiguity, tolerance for 34–7
American Psychological Association (APA) guidelines 152
Andreas, R.E. 80, 112
anthropology, cultural 8, 69, 70, 80
appendix in reports, 66–7, 152, 156–7
Arendt, Hannah 27–8, 35–6, 37, 38
audio-taping 82, 83, 94, 98, 108, 113
    equipment 99, 107, 110, 179
    transcripts *see* transcripts
audit trail 135, 146, 147, 157
Australia 171
autism study 63, 151, 171–7

Bakhtin, M. 37
Becker, H.S. 71
behaviourism 38
Being There (film) 72
Belenky, M. *et al.* 8, 59, 80, 82, 121, 147, 150, 156
    interpretive-descriptive research 44, 122, 123
Benedict, Ruth 69
Bennett, L. 104
Bentz, V.M. 113
Berg, B. 1, 72, 79, 112
Biklen, D. 151, 159, 171, 172–3
Biklen, S. 1, 47, 80, 82, 112, 127
Blieszner, R. 150
Blumer, H. 133
Boas, F. 69

Bogdan, R. 47, 82, 112, 127, 159, *see also* Taylor
Boise, H.E. *et al.* 168
Boucher, M. 171
brainstorming 50, 85, 88
Bronfenbrenner, U. 68
Brown, L.M. 80, 121, 147, 150
Bruner, J. 18, 21, 37–8
Burgess, R. 1

Campbell, D. 7
Camus, A. 36
Carson, Johnny 182
case study approach 47n, 151, 153, 154, 159, 174
categories 85, 87–8, 94, 158
    and coding 127–8, 134–44, 157
    rules for inclusion 138, 139–44
Cerbin, W. 57 ·
Cézanne, Paul 34–5
Chang, H. 45, 150
Chicago school of sociology 8
Chileda Habilitation Institute 171, 175, 176
coding categories 127–8, 134–44, 157
Coles, R. 69
computer programs 148n
Comte, Auguste 3
concept mapping 50–2, 54, 88
confidentiality 94, 100, 108, 154, 176, 179
Corbin, J. 122, 144
Crossley, R. 171, 172, 173
Culley, M. 122
Cummins, R.A. 172

Daly, K. 104
Dartmouth College 112

data
  analysis
    constant comparative method 66,
      126–7, 134–46, 155, 176
    early/ongoing 44, 46–7, 62, 64
    qualitative methods 121–4
      versus traditional 11, 26–7
    in report section 152, 155–6
  collection
    qualitative methods 44–6, 54, 62–6,
      68, 146, 174, 175–6
      versus traditional 11, 16, 26–7
    in report section 152, 155, 169
Denzin, N.K. 69
Desert Storm War 86–7, 106
Dexter, L.A. 79
diagrams and maps 73, 75, 76, 180
Dignity through Education and
  Language (DEAL) 171, 173
discovery 21–2, 132–3, 135, 137
documents
  analysis 66, 69, 129, 146, 176
  collection 46, 68, 110–12, 127
Donnellan, A.M. *et al.* 173
Dornbusch, S.M. 150
Douglas, J. 63
drop-out prevention program 70–1, 121,
  151

Edgerton, R.B. 159
education studies 7, 8, 69, 80, 111
Entwhistle, N. 169
epistemology 3–4, 30, 44, 82, *see also*
  knowledge
Epoche process 123
Erickson, C. 57, 83
Erickson, F. 46, 112
ethics 70
Ethnograph computer program 148n
ethnography 3, 69

Farrell, E. *et al.* 70–1, 75, 121, 151,
  159
feminist theory 7, *see also* women's
  studies
film media 46, 111, 112, 113, 161,
  173
Fisher, Sir Ronald 17
focal awareness 21, 32–3

focus of inquiry
  broadening/narrowing 46–7, 55, 60,
    69
  and categories of meaning 128, 143
  developing a 43–4, 50–5, 63, 87–8
  and researcher's experience 66, 86
  and sampling 56, 57, 59, 60, 62, 63,
    154
  statement 64, 85, 133, 134, 140,
    152–3, 173–4
Fowler, Gene 157
Freud, Sigmund 8, 111
friendships study 95, 103, 130–1, 158

Garber, H.G. 45
gender issues 59–60, 130–1, 144, 155,
  158
Gilgun, J.F. 104
Gilligan, C. 8, 80, 82, 121, 147, 150
Glaser, B.G. 57, 62, 68
  on data analysis 122, 126, 127, 134,
    155, 176
Goertz, J.P. 126, 134
Grene, M. 21, 25, 30, 31–3
Guba, E.G. *see* Lincoln

Habermas, J. 7
Hancock, E. 80, 122
Handel, G. 104
Harbert, E.M. *et al.* 112
Harvard University 8, 82
Heisenberg, W. 7
Hesse, E. 10
Hetherington, E.M. 150
Hodgson, V. 44, 58, 62, 67n
Hogan, S. 154, 155
Holt, J. 69
Huberman, A.M. 127
human as instrument 26–30, 38–9, 46,
  66, 96–7, 107, 155
human plurality 27–9, 37, 38

Ihde, D. 123
implications of study 152, 156, 160
index card system 128, 129–31, 134–9,
  148n, 176
indwelling 5, 25–7, 45, 69, 71, 72
  and human plurality 27–9
  and narrativity 37–8

and tacit knowledge 30–4, 39
and tolerance for ambiguity 34–7
interviews 69, 73, 98–100, 146, 159, 169,
    175–6
  clinical method 8, 82
  group 46, 68, 83, 87, 103–10, 114n
  guide/schedule 81, 83–4, 85–8, 92,
    93–7, 99, 114n
    group 87, 107–8, 109, 110
    in reports 66, 94–5, 156, 178–83
  in-depth 63, 79–81, 102, 128, 150, 161
    and other data collection 46, 68,
      111, 112
  questions *see* questions
  structured 82, 87, 88, 95, 96, 107,
    113–14n
  transcripts *see* transcripts
  unstructured 81–3, 114n
introduction in reports 152, 153, 160,
    178

James, William 111
Jenkins, Glen 167–8, 169–70
Johnson, J.H. 172
journals 111, 122, 152
  researchers' 68–9, 132, 134, 146

Kanner, L. 171
Katz, L. 123
Keller, E. 7
Keynes, J.M. 17
Kidder, L.H. 141
Kincheloe, J. 1, 3
King, M. 3
knowledge
  tacit/explicit 30–4, 36–7, 39, 45
  theory of 11–13, 19, 25, 30, 59,
    see also epistemology
Koegel, P. 159
Konstantareas, N.M. 172
Kozol, J. 69
Krueger, R.A. 104, 106
Kuh, G.D. 80, 112
Kuhn, T. 9, 10
Kuralt, Charles 178–9

LaCrosse, Wisconsin 157, 167, 169–70,
    171
LeCompte, M.D. 126, 134

lectures research 57–8, 59, 61–2, 67n
Lever, J. 111
Levinson, D.J. 122
Lincoln Middle School 77
Lincoln, Y.S. and Guba, E.G.
  access 70, 72
  data analysis 126, 127, 131, 134–9,
    144, 174, 176
  data unitizing 128, 130
  focus of enquiry 44, 50, 53, 54
  human-as-instrument 26–7, 155
  interviews 79, 81, 87, 98
  notes 68
  perspective 124
  research paradigms 9–10, 12, 14, 48
  sampling 57, 58, 62, 64
  trustworthiness 64, 85, 131, 145–7
LISQUAL computer program 148n
logic 3–4
Longfellow Middle School 167–70
Lund, C. 171

McAvity, K. 104
McClurg, K. 86
Mack, J.E. 172
Magolda, M.B. 80
Malinowski, B. 69
maps and diagrams 73, 75, 76, 180
Marshall, J. 128
Marton, F. *et al*. 58, 59
mathematical analysis *see* statistical
Maxwell, J.A. 10
Maykut, P.S. 45, 83, 86, 158, 167, 174,
    178
Maykut, P.S. *et al*. (1992) 101, 128, 130,
    140, 144
Mead, Margaret 69
meaning, concept of 28, 35, 37–9
Measor, L. 113
Melbourne, Australia 171
Meldman, L.S. 44, 156
member checks 147–8
Meno's question 30, 36–7
mentally retarded students study 80, 112
Merleau-Ponty, M. 3, 34
Merton, R.K. *et al*. 82, 114
metaphysics 10
methods section of reports 65, 152,
    153–4, 160, 175–6

Miles, M.B. 127
Mischler, E.G. 71, 80, 98–9, 147
Mohatt, G. 112
Morehouse, R. 28, 30, 86, 167, 178
Morgan, D.L. 103, 104, 105, 106, 114
Moustakas, C. 123
Myres, S.L. 111

narrativity 37–8
New York 70
notes 68, 94, 99–100, 107, 176, 179
 field 73–9, 83, 129, 146, 159, 175
 transcripts 46, 103, 127

objectivity/subjectivity 17, 19–21, 124
observations 111, 127, 146, 175, *see also*
 participant
O'Donohue, R. 10–11, 14
Ogilvy, J. 10, 14
Oishi, S. 171
ontology 3–4
Ortega, J. 29
outcomes
 arriving at 135, 139, 143–4
 case study approach to 47
 reporting 66, 72, 150–62, 169, 174,
 176–7
 reviewing 71–2
 trustworthiness *see* trustworthiness
Oxman, J. 172

paradigms, alternate/traditional 4–5,
 9–10, 18, 38, 45
 and postulates *see* postulates
participant
 activity 32
 as collaborator 70–1
 feedback 122, 147–8, 169
 observation 46, 65, 68, 69–70, 72–9,
 103, 104
 perspectives 47, 82, 88
patriarchy 7, 8
Patton, M. 1, 3, 39n, 69, 72, 123, 127
 on indwelling 27, 29
 on interviews 83, 87, 90–5, 97, 98,
 107
 on sampling 56–7, 65
Payne, S.L. 88
peer debriefers 147, 174

Perry, W.G. 8, 59, 80, 82, 121, 150
Persian Gulf War 86–7, 106
perspectives 14, 16, 19–21, 124, 169, 178
 participant 47, 82, 88
Petersen, A.C. 150
phenomenology 3, 4–5, 11–15, 20, 34,
 123
photocopying 127–8, 129, 143, 176
photographs 46, 111, 112
Piaget, Jean 8, 82
Plato 30
Polanyi, M. 3, 15–16, 17, 21
 on indwelling 25–7, 29–33, 39, 69, 72
positivism 3, 4–5, 7, 10–15, 18, 26, 39
poster session 161–2
postmodernism 7, 22n
postulates of research paradigms 4–5,
 9–16, 18, 20–2&n, 28, 37, 53, 55,
 56, 155
 table 12
postures 5, 25
Prior, M.P. 172
probes 95–6, 97, 107, 109
problem statement 63–4, 152, 171–3
propositional statement 139–41, 142–4,
 158, 159, 160
Prosch, H. 3
psychology 8, 10, 38, 70, 71, 80, 111,
 152

qualitative research characteristics chart
 48
questions, interview 88–90
 open-ended/closed 82, 88, 90, 93, 94,
 107
 probes *see* probes
 typology 90–5, 107

reactivity 155
reading and writing 38–9
references in reports 66, 152, 156
research
 design 43–4, 63–5, 69, 123, 144
 in reports 152–3, 154, 155, 160,
 174, 175
 teamwork 131–2, 133, 134, 136, 144,
 146–7, 155, 160–1
Rico, C.L. 85
Rogers, C. 8

Index

Roman Catholics study 154, 155
Rose, S.M. 158

Saljo, R. 44
sampling 45, 56–63, 65, 109, 152, 154
  maximum variation 56–62, 65, 175
  purposive 45, 56, 58, 59, 65, 175
    profile 61–2
  random 45, 56, 57
  size 62–3, 65
  snowball 57
  theoretical 57
Schafer, R. 86
Schlissel, L. 111
Scholes, R. 38–9
school climate study 63, 167–70
Schumacher, E.F. 28
Schwartz, P. 10, 14
Schwartz, S. 172
science 16, 152
  history of 3, 7–10, 17
  philosophy of 30
  sociology of 9
Sellars, Peter 72
Shils, E.A. 70
Sibbet, D. 84, 85, 126
Silver, P. 29
Simons, J. 171
slide show 161
Smith, R.M. et al. 168
Smuksta, M. 111
social sciences 8, 69, 80, 111, 112, 152
Socrates 30
Stake, R. 7, 44
statistical/mathematical analysis 2, 17,
    18, 21, 26, 62, 126
Stenhouse, L. 113
Stewart, M. 112
Stoddart, K. 72
Strauss, A.L. 57, 62, 68
  on data analysis 122, 126, 127, 134,
    144, 155, 176
Stromberg, R. 3
students, studies of
  college 8, 80, 82, 107–8, 133, 139–40,
    see also lectures; television
  school 69, 70–1, 83, 112, 121, 151, 161

subjectivity/objectivity 17, 19–21, 124
Syracuse University 171

Taylor, S.
  and Bogdan, R. 57, 68, 70, 73, 81,
    126, 132, 139, 141
  Bogdan, R. and 1, 18, 34, 36, 80
teleology 3–4
television study 94–5, 112, 178–83
theory building 122, 126
transcripts 8, 129, 146
  of audio-tapes 46, 71, 100–3, 110,
    127, 169, 176
trustworthiness of outcomes 64, 85, 131,
    145–7, 152–3, 156, 174
typing 100, 103, 127

unitizing data 128–31, 134, 142–3, 146,
    176
USA 8, 45, 70, 82, 111, 150
  war veterans 86–7, 106

Valle, R. 3
Van Wright, G. 36
video-taping 46, 111, 112, 113, 173
Vidulich, D. 148
Viterbo College 169, 171, 178
Vonnegut, Kurt 157

Wagner, J. 46
war veterans' study 86–7, 106
Wax, R.H. 123–4
Webster, C.D. et al. 172
Whitbourne, S.K. 80
Wilson, J. 46
Wing, L. 173
Wisconsin 157, 167, 169–70, 171
Wolcott, H.F. 155, 160
women's studies 8, 44, 80, 111, 113,
    121, 147
words and action 18–19, 27–8, 35, 46,
    47, 68, 128
writing
  and reading 38–9
  reports 145, 151–2, 156, 157, 158,
    159–60, 161

Fundamentals of Educational Research
Gary Anderson, *McGill University, Canada*

Search and Re-Search:
What the Inquiring Teacher Needs to Know
Edited by Rita S. Brause, *Fordham University, USA* and John S. Mayher,
New York University, USA

Doing Qualitative Research:
Circles Within Circles
Margot Ely, *New York University, USA* with Margaret Anzul,
Teri Friedman, Diane Garner and Ann McCormack Steinmetz

Teachers as Researchers:
Qualitative Inquiry as a Path to Empowerment
Joe L. Kincheloe, *Clemson University, USA*

Key Concepts for Understanding Curriculum
Colin Marsh, *Secondary Education Authority, Western Australia*

Mike Boulton

300.72
MAY

Beginning Qualitative Research
A Philosophic and Practical Guide